MW00453552

PRESCOTT'S
ORIGINAL
WHISKEY ROW

BRADLEY G. COURTNEY

THE
History
PRESS

Published by The History Press
Charleston, SC
www.historypress.net

Copyright © 2015 by Bradley G. Courtney
All rights reserved

Front cover: Palace Saloon interior, circa 1901. *Courtesy of Sharlot Hall Museum.*
Back cover: South Montezuma Street showing the Pacific Brewery next to the Arizona Miner
office, 1880s. *Courtesy of Sharlot Hall Museum.*

First published 2015

Manufactured in the United States

ISBN 978.1.46711.767.8

Library of Congress Control Number: 2015949291

Notice: The information in this book is true and complete to the best of our knowledge. It is
offered without guarantee on the part of the author or The History Press. The author and
The History Press disclaim all liability in connection with the use of this book.

All rights reserved. No part of this book may be reproduced or transmitted in any form
whatsoever without prior written permission from the publisher except in the case of brief
quotations embodied in critical articles and reviews.

Contents

Acknowledgements   5
Preface   7

1. Prelude to the Birth of Whiskey Row   9
2. The Real Quartz Rock and the Diana Saloon:
   Mothers of Whiskey Row   20
3. Law and Order, and Lawlessness, Along the Emergent
   Whiskey Row   35
4. The "Cabinet": The Heartbeat of Early Whiskey Row   43
5. The Montezuma, Jackson & Tompkins' and Keystone
   Saloons: Contributors to Whiskey Row's Growing Notoriety   53
6. Early Beer Breweries of Whiskey Row: A Short History   67
7. Whiskey Row's Embellishment Wars and the James
   Dodson Era   80
8. Ellis and Whitney's Palace Saloon and the Whiskey Row
   Fire of 1883   91
9. The Whiskey Row of Montezuma Street Takes Shape   98
10. Arizona's Most Famous Saloon Story: The Legend of Chance
    Cobweb Hall and the True Story of Violet "Baby Bell" Hicks   114
11. Buckey O'Neill, the Rough Riders and Whiskey Row   126
12. Prelude to the Death of Whiskey Row   133

Notes   137
About the Author   144

Acknowledgements

First, thanks to my many outdoor offices in the Prescott National Forest where the only distraction was beauty and the sound of wind scuttling through the pines. Second, thank you to Noelle, my Shih Tzu, who gave me constant companionship along the way. On the human side, there isn't enough space to list all who merit my gratitude. There is Dan Thomas, my spiritual brother, who sat with me during an untold number of Pine Wind campfires as we worked out life according to the way we understood the Word of God and how it applied to the circumstances affecting our respective lives. Such discourse goes beyond books. There are my "children," Joshua and Lindsay "Bird" Courtney, who as adults I'm completely proud of and overwhelmingly happy to call my friends. This book wouldn't have been possible without my parents. Bob Courtney sparked a love for history that burns stronger in me every waking day. Bertha Courtney's steadfast love still carries me. Thank you to my "Auntie Care" Hogberg, whose passion for local history preservation is inspiring. Local historians and history advocates worthy of my thanks are too many to mention, but most—not all—are found in my endnotes. Nancy Burgess deserves special thanks for donating several historic photos and for her encouragement. My gratitude is oversized for Brenda "OK Girl" Taylor and her wonderful staff at the Sharlot Hall Museum Library and Archives, the best of its kind in the entire Southwest. Wednesdays, Thursdays and Fridays there, four hours each shot month after month, are cherished memories. Thank you to The History Press, especially the ever-positive Megan Laddusaw.

ACKNOWLEDGEMENTS

My highest and best thanks are reserved for the love of my life, Holly Courtney. If you are one of the blessed few who knows what it's like to know there is no other able to fulfill that need we all have to love and be loved, then you know words fail but are also worth the striving. Holly has also played the role of proofreader, critic and always willing listener.

To the handful of people I love so very much (you know who you are), remember grace, and remember this: although I am the happiest person I know—which is "bully"—I'd rather it be you.

Preface

Whiskey Row of Prescott, Arizona, is one of the true landmarks of the historic and present-day American West. Walking its sidewalks today feels like a refreshing step back in time. But it is more. It's what the West has become. It's where the West is going. The Whiskey Row of today is neither an anachronism nor a contradiction but a symbol of the struggle to fuse the present to the past. Such is not an easy task. *Prescott's Original Whiskey Row* is an attempt to assist that never-ending process along and help that union become more complete.

Whiskey Row's history has been presented in random spurts over the years—a newspaper or magazine article here, a chapter or mention in a book there, the setting for a journal essay or popular history piece. Yet it has never been the sole subject of a book, even though Whiskey Row is central to Prescott history and, in a sense, Arizona history. It served as the social center of the capital of Arizona Territory during two separate stretches—1864–67 and 1877–89. Whiskey Row was, and still is, the heart of Prescott.

It's been said that, except for a few battlefield exploits here and there, the history of the West was written in saloons. Indeed, much of Prescott's history can be taught through its earliest saloons. What was once almost furtively called Whiskey Row was a world unto itself, had a culture of its own and, with its true events and real people, was a microcosm of the frontier west. Furthermore, Whiskey Row's history is more than a frivolous journey into the romantic Wild West, although there's indeed more of that type of allure and excitement attached to it than most frontier locales.

Whiskey Row of Prescott, Arizona, is one of the true landmarks of both the historic and present-day American West. *Norman Fisk.*

Whiskey Row is nowadays famous throughout the Southwest, but its history demonstrates it should be even more so. This book covers its first thirty-six years. It begins with the first saloons of Prescott, which coincided with Prescott's birth in 1864, and concludes with the onset of the Great Fire of 1900. Three-and-a-half years of extensive and intensive research and analysis back this study. Along the way, legends I hoped would prove true sometimes did. Sometimes they didn't. The truths they were based on, however, didn't disappoint, at least in terms of proving fascinating, as did the manner in which they became legends. Indeed, the unfermented truth is sometimes more flavorsome than the cocktailed legend—but there's no denying the let-down the rectified versions of history sometimes rendered. There are also several newly revealed historical events that transpired on Whiskey Row delineated herein that might've worked themselves into legends over time had there been exploitive writers in Prescott between 1864 and 1900. Dime novelists would have done very well on Whiskey Row.

Chapter 1

Prelude to the Birth of Whiskey Row

The history of Prescott's famous Whiskey Row begins with trees. Wood, that is. It was born and raised in wood. It prospered in wood, struggled to stay alive because of wood and finally died in wood. Some early inhabitants of Prescott observed that while the structures of many towns in the Southwest were often made of adobe, most of Prescott's buildings were constructed entirely of wood. This was a huge fire risk anywhere, but especially in an area prone to drought. Furthermore, within Prescott's inner verve, many edifices were connected to one another, creating the effect of one long, continuous house. In dry spells, it became an enormous tinderbox.

In the summer of 1900, it was just that. A single candle-dripped spark quickly swelled into a conflagration of nearly mythical dimensions and intensity. Yet, because of a never-give-up frontier spirit, Prescott and Whiskey Row became the true phoenixes of Arizona. Both would rise from literal flames and wooden ashes, both would resurrect stronger and more impressive and both would not only endure but also thrive.

Although the "Big Fire" or "Great Fire" of July 14, 1900, was a virtual holocaust, it signaled both the death and consequent rebirth of Whiskey Row. What about Whiskey Row's original birth and evolution? To acquire an understanding of its roots and earliest history, a summary understanding of Prescott's dawn is required. In 1864, the founding fathers of Arizona trekked from the East and Midwest in search of a proper setting to establish a government in the recently declared Arizona Territory. They were led by John Goodwin, an Ohioan who'd been appointed territorial governor by

President Abraham Lincoln after his first appointee, John Gurley, died before taking office. William Hinkling Prescott's epic literary work, *The History of the Conquest of Mexico*, had sparked the imaginations of several members of the governor's party, who wanted to not only set up a government but also find fortune themselves in a region they surmised might've been once occupied by rich Aztecs. That expanse today is called the Central Arizona Highlands, an area then proving to possess vast mineral sources.

After a brief sojourn fifteen miles north in Chino Valley, the "promised land" emerged when Goodwin's group eventually reached a semi-level section situated in the midst of one of the world's largest ponderosa pine forests. Within this largely unexplored area, there was little else but mountain wildlife, some indigenous people and a few transplanted, daring souls already risking it all in hopes of achieving a new and prosperous life. Therein also existed a seemingly endless supply of natural source material for building a town. In this picturesque environment rose a hamlet that would quickly become a town and eventually a city. Prescott would become early Arizona's irrefutable historical heart and soul. And the heart and soul of Prescott would become known throughout the West as Whiskey Row.

Robert Groom was primarily responsible for drawing up plans that would begin to make Prescott a real town with streets that formed blocks which could be divided into lots. A resolution was also made to reserve "at least one square in the proposed town site for a public plaza." That area exists today as the Yavapai County Courthouse Plaza, which, in 2008, was named one of America's top ten public spaces by the American Planning Association, a list that includes New York City's Central Park and Washington, D.C.'s Union Station. The Plaza is an important part of Whiskey Row history.

The town was soon named after William Prescott, the preeminent historian admired by many in the governor's party. Two of Prescott's most relevant streets—Montezuma and Cortez—were named for historic personages related to the Spanish conquest of the Aztec Empire of Mexico. Whiskey Row's Montezuma Street was named after Moctezuma II, the ninth Aztec emperor, whose leadership expanded the Aztec empire to its greatest size. It was during his reign that the Spanish conquistador Hernando Cortés led an expedition that brought down that powerful dynasty and killed Moctezuma II. The street—spelled "Cortez"—running to the east of and directly parallel to Montezuma was named after this conquistador, linking the two enemies forever. However, in spite of Hernando Cortés's historic supremacy, Moctezuma II remains supreme in the Whiskey Row story. The street named for him became the dominant, most vibrant thoroughfare of

Above: In 1864, Prescott's founders created a plaza that today is one of the top public spaces in America. *Norman Fisk.*

Right: Gurley Street is named after John Gurley, who died before he could serve as Arizona Territory's first governor. *Wikimedia Commons.*

Prescott. Today, what Beale Street is to Memphis or Bourbon Street to New Orleans, Montezuma Street's Whiskey Row is to Prescott.[1]

However, Whiskey Row, as it morphed into one version and then another throughout its early history and even after it was rebuilt in 1901, was more than the quarter-city block sectioned off today for visitors on Montezuma Street between Gurley and Goodwin Streets. It was a general area. Early Whiskey Row included all of Prescott's infamous "Block 13"—also called the 100 block—which showcased the north–south positioned Montezuma Street; Montezuma Street was indeed always the center of Whiskey Row. Running parallel to Montezuma was Granite Street, which bordered Prescott's main waterway, Granite Creek. Granite Street's history is perhaps even more notorious than Montezuma's. The east–west streets of Block 13 were named after Arizona Territory's first two governors: Gurley Street after the first appointed governor, John Gurley, to the north, and Goodwin Street to the south, after John Goodwin, the first Lincoln appointee to actually serve as governor in Arizona Territory. Whiskey Row also often spilled over on to Cortez Street, as well as east and west along Gurley and Goodwin Streets. Saloons lined and sometimes dotted these streets, extending the area characterized as Whiskey Row.[2]

SHANTIES, PLANK BARS AND WHISKEY: PRESCOTT'S FIRST SALOONS

The moniker "Whiskey Row" didn't appear in print until 1883, after many of the buildings on Block 13's Montezuma Street had burned to the ground during one of the several major fires that would plague Prescott. Around early Prescott, however, the name had been commonly used for several years prior. How far back can the history of Whiskey Row be taken? The answer is, as far back as the birth of Prescott itself, the year 1864; the wilderness capital soon became accompanied by wilderness saloons. The most frequent story told regarding the saloon that birthed Whiskey Row involves an enterprising pioneer named Isaac Goldberg and his makeshift saloon called the "Quartz Rock." It's one of a handful of Whiskey Row legends that, after persistent retelling, has often been perceived as true history. Like most legends, the Quartz Rock tale has an amusing flavor to it, as well as intriguing characters. It's an endearing and enduring piece of Prescott folklore that is a combination of certain true, distinct events and characters.

BIG BLAZE IN PRES-COTT.

Whisky Row Licked up by Flames.

Hundreds Houseless and Homeless.

Loss about $100,000.

The first time "Whisky Row" appeared in print was in July 1883, after much of it had burned to the ground. *Sharlot Hall Museum.*

The story begins with Goldberg improvising a makeshift cantina, a shanty covering a crude, wooden-board counter, two bottles of whiskey and a single tin-cup, somewhere along the banks of Granite Creek. There's a noseless, AWOL soldier who, depending on the version, is Goldberg's assistant or Goldberg himself. One account has Goldberg initially operating on Granite Street just behind Montezuma Street. Some reputable Prescott historians pinpoint his business as actually having been set up near the southern end of today's Prescott city limits, near where Montezuma now becomes White Spar Road. Regardless, Granite Creek is the central feature to both versions and the key to the legend itself.

Goldberg's immediate success was guaranteed. Miners sought escape by intoxication from the toil of making a living in the surrounding mountains.

He soon ran into problems when inebriated patrons became disoriented from gazing at the trickling water of Granite Creek. Some, it was said, fell into the creek trying to cross on an improvised bridge. Consequently, the proprietor moved his business—once again depending on the rendering— either one street east or north from the outside of town, to Montezuma Street, putting a more suitable distance between his liquor business and the stream. The relocated cantina, it is theorized, was the seed that eventually sprouted a crop of saloons which would later be famously dubbed "Whisky Row" and, later, "Whiskey Row" after the latter spelling of that puissant beverage became the accepted form.

Unlike many legends replete with adornments and contortions of the truth, the Quartz Rock legend is merely a distortion of it. Was Prescott's first saloon a plank bar? It appears that's the most likely scenario, even though it wasn't called the Quartz Rock. There *was* an Isaac Goldberg who in 1894 told his story to the Society of Arizona Pioneers. After spending time in La Paz, a short-lived southwestern Arizona Territory town situated next to the Colorado River, he arrived in the Prescott area during the early spring of 1864, just when a functional territorial government was being set in motion. Goldberg did indeed set up a saloon of sorts, with a "rude counter which concealed sundry bottles of whiskey." This wooden board supported only two bottles, just as the legend claims. Goldberg served his whiskey by the dram dripped into a tin cup.

Goldberg wasn't noseless but his assistant, or "bar-keeper," was a soldier whose nose was indeed mostly missing. This man had deserted an unspecified post (most likely of the Confederate army of the Civil War) but, according to Goldberg, was "a brave man." Goldberg didn't divulge the name of his bartender but said he took good care of him by providing board, shelter and $100 per month.

Goldberg never mentioned a creek or even being near one. As noted earlier, however, some local historians place Goldberg's original "saloon" on lower Granite Creek, just a few miles north of today's Prescott National Forest boundary, to be more accessible to mining locales. This may be true. Goldberg shared a story that inferred his business wasn't exactly "downtown," or at the very least, it demonstrated just how vulnerable original Prescottonians were now that they, in essence, had become part of the wilderness. Early Prescott blended with the surrounding wilderness to the point of barely being discernible from it. Enabling men to become inebriated in such an environment wasn't always an ideal situation.

One morning after a busy night, Goldberg found himself under the gunpoint of "a rough customer" with "blood-shot eyes." The visitor's intentions were clearly unfriendly. Goldberg, however, had a near-full cup of whiskey in his hand, which he dashed into the eyes of this would-be pirate, temporarily blinding him. Goldberg and his assistant then overpowered the ruffian and threw him into their "chamber of penance," which Goldberg described as a frail "adjacent log-pen." The prisoner soon escaped. Angered and still drunk, the amateur outlaw pined for vengeance and hunted for the whiskey sellers, but both had disappeared into the pines. Later, when the man sobered and Goldberg had returned, he sunk into compunction and came by to apologize for his "meanness." So it was, often, along the Central Arizona Highlands frontier. Goldberg asserted, "Thus we Pioneers of Arizona were afflicted by desperadoes—foes frequently as dreadful as the detested and dangerous aborigines."[3]

Goldberg never disclosed a name for his business. It's likely it bore no appellation at all. Yet he may have actually honchoed Prescott's first wholesale/retail liquor business, if not saloon. Also, Goldberg did indeed move his business into the heart of the six-month-old town, but probably not to Montezuma Street. In the thirteenth *Arizona Weekly Miner*, Prescott's first newspaper (hereafter referred to as the *Miner*), dated September 13, 1864, Goldberg advertised his enterprise for the first time, the first Prescott liquor wholesaler/retailer to do so. He was now selling his wares out of the "Juniper House." This is an intriguing juxtaposition.[4]

The Juniper House, although not a pure saloon, merits attention because of its association with whiskey-man Isaac Goldberg. It was founded by a multifaceted pioneer named George Barnard, who, like Goldberg, had journeyed up from La Paz. Barnard, a native Michigander, was one of several original Prescottonians who initially made his way west after hearing of the discovery of gold on Sutter Creek in California. Like several other 1849 Argonauts, he later moved to Arizona after learning of mineral strikes there.[5]

The Juniper House bore a remarkably similar history to that of Goldberg's cantina venture. It also serves as an exemplar of how the first service-oriented businesses were built, using the resources readily available. Less than a year prior, where there were only a few human beings present, there was now a semi-village anxiously hurrying to be not only a real town but also the political and commercial center of Arizona Territory. When Prescott's first Fourth of July rolled around, with the Civil War still raging and the future of the United States still hanging in the balance, it was critical for these first Prescottonians, overwhelmingly pro-Union, to celebrate it properly. For entrepreneurs, it was time to get a provisional business in place to open on the Fourth and think long term later.

Named "by the boys" because of the sizable juniper tree by which Barnard conducted his business, the Juniper House was undeniably Prescott's first hotel as well as its first food and beverage go-to spot. It, too, began in the most pioneer of ways. One witness noted that the "progressively inclined" Barnard had "no house nor stove" when he opened for business on the first Independence Day in Prescott. Rather, he cooked his cuisine over an open campfire by that juniper tree. Customers found it convenient that after their repasts were dished out, they could move to the shady side of the tree to more comfortably enjoy them. Eventually, nail and lumber sheltered a workable restaurant and hotel, where Goldberg's liquors provided a welcome addition.[6]

When July 4th rolled around, Barnard was ready to go. He served breakfast, lunch and dinner; his bill of fare featured various beef, mutton and venison recipes. Barnard's menu was a hit, as the Juniper House was "largely patronized" that day. All of this was reputedly cooked over a campfire. There were more dishes offered than what was reported. From another noteworthy pioneer, Charles Genung, Barnard purchased sixty-two pounds of elderberries at a dollar a pound from him for the event, with which he made numerous pies to sell. They were also used as currency. Barnard had employed brothers Jacob and Sam Miller to haul logs to the site where he planned to erect his restaurant, and paid them in elderberry pies.[7]

A pencil-drawn map, dated 1864—stored in the Sharlot Hall Museum Library and Archives of Prescott—shows a log structure labeled "Juniper House" standing on the southeast corner of Cortez and Goodwin Streets, one block from the area sectioned off today on Montezuma Street and labeled Whiskey Row. Although most likely drawn from memory by an original Prescottonian many years later, the drawing representing the Juniper House does indeed fit the description of it by another pioneer named Albert Banta. Although he depicted the original restaurant portion of the Juniper House as being "a spacious dining hall," in reality it was a twelve-by fifteen-foot room constructed from pine logs. A single table made from halved logs placed side-by-side, flat sides up, was featured in the middle of the room. The riven pine presented a problem for prissier patrons: "The pitch oozed in gobs from the split surface of the pine poles, and one had to have a care lest his bread or other things got stuck in the pitch."[8]

The first two Prescott saloons mentioned in print were those run by John Roundtree and John Dickson. Both were unnamed and temporary, primarily set up for the town's first major celebration on Prescott's first Fourth of July. Both got the job done. Dickson even had a billiard table brought in for the occasion, the first in Prescott. It was a momentous event, with every one of the four hundred or so "Prescottites" in attendance, consisting mostly, if not totally, of men. Both "saloons were crowded with customers, and we will not say how much whiskey was disposed of—it might surprise our temperate friends from Tucson and La Paz. Nobody was hurt, although the boys waxed very merry, and some of them very tipsy, and there was no little promiscuous firing of revolvers."[9]

Roundtree's saloon—actually a partnership with a doctor also referred to as a "judge," J.T. Alsop—was not unlike the Juniper House and Goldberg's original whiskey shop in the way it was set up. Quickly constructed near south Montezuma Street, the roof was a mere covered-wagon canvas cloth stretched over two pine poles. The bar itself was nothing more than a ten-gallon keg filled with what one pioneer thought might be whiskey—at least that is what those present decided to call it. Roundtree's saloon may've been the first to be located on Montezuma Street. It was not sited, however, on the section of Montezuma between Gurley and Goodwin Streets that is today's Whiskey Row but between Carleton Street to the south and Goodwin.[10]

By October of that year, Roundtree partnered with Thomas Hodges to establish the first Prescott saloon to bear an actual name: "Their new saloon, 'The Pine Grove,' [is] in full blast, with abundant liquors and a billiard table." It was situated on Cortez Street. One of Prescott's most notable and successful pioneers, Edmund Wells, asserted that the Pine Grove was the town's first "regulated saloon" and that Hodges—who often bartered his liquors for "cigars and services"—was the principal proprietor.[11]

How long the Pine Grove stayed in business is unknown. It would soon be overshadowed by Prescott's first saloon of lasting significance, one founded by a genuine mover and shaker during Arizona Territory's earliest years, William Hardy. His bar was none other than the "Quartz Rock." The true Quartz Rock would go on to create its own chapter in Whiskey Row history.

First, however, a general understanding and categorization of early Whiskey Row saloons is in order.

EARLY WHISKEY ROW'S FIVE TIERS

With a few exceptions, the saloons of early Whiskey Row can be divided into five tiers. The top tier is composed of just two, the Cabinet and Palace saloons. That's because they're the only pre–Great Fire saloons still standing; their histories are still ongoing, albeit in one form as the Palace Restaurant and Saloon. Even when separate institutions, they were the game-changing, trend-setting saloons of their time. Today, the Palace and the beautiful Jersey Lilly Saloon—formerly the post-1900 second-floor hotel area of the Palace—stand tall together as the centerpiece of Whiskey Row.

The second tier is composed of the Quartz Rock, Diana, Montezuma and Jackson & Tompkins' saloons. Like the Cabinet and Palace, these were often *the* places to be, socialize, do business, play games or just enjoy a favorite spirited beverage. Except for the Quartz Rock, they all had fifteen-plus years of relatively continuous business. Expansion, improvements and embellishments were common and frequent goals, if only as efforts to match the Cabinet and Palace. The first and second-tier saloons all attracted a top-heavy share of patronage. This was both good and bad. They were often the subjects or sites of local news, gossip and stories that were amusing, romantic and, unfortunately, sometimes tragic. Attracting more people produced not only more commerce but sometimes more trouble: robberies, brawls, shootings and murders. They also featured gambling, which was as much a part of the lifeblood of the Old West as saloons and whiskey. Finally, their accommodations and products were usually more diverse and of higher quality. All in all, the saloons of tiers one and two dominate the history of Whiskey Row. For that reason, one more saloon can be added to this tier, the Keystone Saloon. Although not a "*the* place to be" kind of saloon, the Keystone's unique history makes it a second-tier saloon.

Third-tier saloons were worthy competitors of first and second-tier saloons but never made quite the same splash. If they made the local news, it was usually to laud improvements made or adornments added. For the most part, they avoided the conflicts and tragedies the more dominant saloons hosted, which in some ways made third-tier saloons more attractive; perhaps that was one reason they experienced steady business and often endured much like top-tier Whiskey Row cantinas. This level includes the Parlor, Cob Web Hall, the Nifty, Exchange, Eclipse, Bit, Union, Plaza Bit, Fashion, Sazerac, Keg, Cate's, Barrett's and Capitol saloons.

Fourth-tier saloons were plentiful and basically "get the job done"–type locales. They were well-kept watering holes that may or may not have advertised: drinks were served, cigars smoked, perhaps a bit of gambling. Subsumed here are the Pine Tree, Royal, Gem, Headquarters, Nugget, Arcade, Prescott, Phoenix, Central, Hughey's, Kearney's, Empire, Petrified, Maier's, Tivoli, Owl and several undocumented saloons. There were also saloons connected to other businesses: bakeries, restaurants, lodging houses or hotels and even grocery and mercantile stores. They were fourth-tier establishments as well.

Then there was the Champion Saloon, a lowly tier unto itself. No other bar in Prescott ever received the type of negative publicity the Champion did. Its lack of quality was news in itself. Yet it refused to go away. Robert Connell, a shrewd businessman who, in the 1870s and early '80s, held a near monopoly on wholesale liquor sales in Prescott, owned the Champion. Salooning was a secondary endeavor. He supplied much of the alcoholic beverages to Whiskey Row saloons. His Champion Saloon, however, at the corner of Montezuma and Goodwin Streets, was a dive and could only be entered via Whiskey Row Alley between Montezuma and Granite Streets. When it was repainted in 1876, it reminded onlookers "of fellows we have seen wearing clean collars and dirty socks." Connell, however, had some pride; this description must've stung. In August 1877, the Champion was put through a complete refitting. However, it remained a clandestine operation.[12]

In a separate category were Prescott's beer breweries. The Arizona Brewery, Pacific Brewery, Arcade Brewery and City Brewery, which later became the Excelsior Brewery, were some of the finest in Arizona Territory if not the West.

Of the first saloons, two had more impact on the growth of Whiskey Row than the others: the real Quartz Rock and its younger sister, the Diana Saloon. They were the true mothers of Whiskey Row.

Chapter 2

The Real Quartz Rock and the Diana Saloon

Mothers of Whiskey Row

The Quartz Rock/Isaac Goldberg legend has had long-lasting and pervasive effects on presentations of Whiskey Row history, especially regarding its origins. Even the famous Palace Restaurant and Saloon, the oldest still-standing saloon in Arizona, has been incorrectly linked to Goldberg. As revealed in chapter one, the actual establishment wherein Goldberg eventually hawked his wares was George Barnard's Juniper House, not the Quartz Rock. The Juniper House slowly floundered and then met its demise in 1865 after falling victim to the first of the many destructive fires that would plague Prescott and Whiskey Row. Some believed the Juniper House was already on its way out because Barnard was too munificent and trusting toward his customers. Perhaps because he was not only the restaurant's chef but also the entire culinary department and service staff, he didn't have the time or means to check whether a patron had paid and therefore wound up preparing and serving too many meals for free. Barnard, among many other accomplishments, later co-founded one of Whiskey Row's most long-lasting bars, the Nifty Saloon on Montezuma Street.[13]

There are five establishments qualified to vie for the distinction of being Prescott's first legitimate saloon. This list includes the actual Quartz Rock. Ironically, in the same *Miner* wherein Goldberg had taken out an advertisement announcing that his dramshop was now being run from the Juniper House, it was revealed that the venerable pioneer William Hardy would soon be establishing businesses in Prescott. Hardy, born and raised in New York but in his heart a southern Arizona man, was an unstoppable

NIFTY SALOON.

AT THE "NIFTY," ON MONTEZUMA ST.,

THE THIRSTY CAN

GET GOOD WHISKEY,

RUM, GIN, BRANDY, KUMMEL,

SWEET OR SOUR WINES,

And Tolerable Water. Drop In.

Thos. Farrell is prepared to furnish HOT OR COLD LUNCHES, at the Nifty Saloon, at all hours of the day or night.
sep20tf.

One of the Nifty Saloon's attractions was water that could be tolerated. *Sharlot Hall Museum.*

entrepreneur. Among his various accomplishments, he founded the lower Colorado River town Hardyville, which later became Bullhead City. The *Miner* indicated, however, that Hardy had "lately made a hurried visit to Prescott with a view of opening a business establishment here." He recognized that with the founding of the territorial capital in the recently created Prescott, it would soon be a center of considerable commerce and activity and harbor the advantages of accommodating the government. It didn't hurt that Fort Whipple and its soldiers were also now nearby and that the area would soon be teeming with even more miners needing a place to gather and let loose socially.[14]

Hardy actually had two businesses planned. Just as George Barnard had done prior to erecting the historic Juniper House, Hardy employed the Miller brothers to haul logs to the lots on which they would be built. At first, the denizens of Prescott didn't know exactly what he had in mind except that one would be a store offering "a miscellaneous assortment of goods" and that they would be on the east side of Granite Street. Within two months, townsfolk learned Hardy's second business would be a saloon. When time for its grand opening neared, Hardy and his associates enticed customers by publicizing that on-the-house samples of a new quality of libations would be offered.[15]

On November 14, 1864, Hardy, with great ceremony, opened his bar. Attending this inauguration was an extemporarily established local club of townsmen. With tongues plainly planted in the corners of their respective mouths, they called themselves the "Barbarians." Their mission was to "properly [celebrate] important events" that marked Prescott's progress. The Barbarians were led by Judge William Berry. Members included Governor John Goodwin himself, Secretary Richard McCormick and several officers from Fort Whipple. On this night, their "celebration" was three-fold. Opening a bar featuring the best billiard table in the territory and offering "a better class of liquors than we have been used to in Prescott" was certainly, in their minds, significant progress. There was also the completion of the territory's first legislative session to commemorate, which had concluded four days prior. The grand opening of Hardy's saloon was considered Prescott's first "soiree." The local population was heavily lopsided with males, but on this occasion, almost a dozen ladies were present with whom the gentlemen danced the night away.[16]

There was another momentous event for the Barbarians to memorialize. The first marriage to be held in Prescott wedded Arizona's first speaker of the house, William Claude Jones, to Caroline Stephens, who arrived with her family in Prescott on October 5 from Texas. A shivaree was in order. The whirlwind wedding had taken place on November 13, the night before the Quartz Rock opened. When members of the new territorial government learned of Jones's marriage, they were shocked—and seemingly amused— that Jones's bride was but fifteen years old—thought to be forty years his junior. Needless to say, Jones became the butt of some frontier jocosity and thus the Barbarians' first victim.

Jones was quite knowledgeable about the assumed history of the new territory, especially regarding what was thought to be the influence of Aztec civilization upon it. Earlier, he'd been asked to give a series of public lectures on the subject, which he did. It would come back to haunt him. The Barbarians poked fun at Jones by attesting that he, like the Aztec men he admired, had courted "a young virgin" and that he'd been "permitted to roam about of nights, and make the acquaintance of parents who had marriageable daughters," like the Aztecs of old.

Before the Barbarians made their way to the newlyweds' house, they grabbed all the "inharmonious instruments" they could carry. Judge Berry led the mock serenade with "a huge piece of sheet iron, upon which he beat most lustily with a crooked club." Secretary McCormick "whipped a bar of steel," while the governor hid in a thicket and beat incessantly on a tin pan. Neither the bride nor groom surfaced right away, so the Barbarians forced their way into the house and "shook hands with the groom and kissed the bride." The teenage bride was sobbing uncontrollably and "panting with fright," which caused the Barbarians to depart and march straight over to Hardy's saloon to celebrate its opening. Mr. and Mrs. Jones bolted to Tucson within the next few days and didn't return to Prescott until April 1865. Jones disappeared from Prescott on May 5, abandoning his young wife, and never returned.[17]

William Claude Jones, speaker of the house, was roasted by the Barbarians after marrying a fifteen-year-old girl. *Wikimedia Commons.*

For three weeks more, the first Granite Street bar was simply called "Hardy's new billiard room" or "saloon." It "attract[ed] much attention," something that'd never been said about the other saloons in town at that time. On December 14, 1864, the public would learn its name: the Quartz Rock. Although Hardy owned this property, he was never an actual Prescott resident. An Irishman, John Bourke, originally ran the Quartz Rock. Bourke was one reason the Quartz Rock immediately became a "popular resort." This was only the beginning for this Irishman, who later instituted the Prescott Hotel. After that he served two terms as sheriff of Yavapai County, followed by an election to the post of county recorder. Unfortunately, Bourke, whose intellect was said to be "of the highest order," was gone too soon. He died at the age of forty-one on March 6, 1868. His memorial service took place on a miserably rainy day, yet nearly every citizen of Prescott attended.[18]

Both of Bourke's bartenders became prominent influences on Whiskey Row history. One, nicknamed "Doc," was Andrew Moeller. Why he was

The Quartz Rock was the first Prescott saloon to advertise on a weekly basis.
Sharlot Hall Museum.

often called "Dr. Moeller" is a mystery. He would become not only a major Whiskey Row figure but also one of the all-time great property magnates of Prescott. The other was Joe Crane. The "jovial" Crane would follow Moeller in another groundbreaking saloon venture and become one of early Whiskey Row's most beloved bar-keepers and proprietors.[19]

As divulged in chapter one, the Quartz Rock legend is a mixture of true events and characters. What about that part of the legend consistently repeated, that after many had become sick from the sight of Granite Creek's running water or had fallen into it after a few too many drinks, the Quartz Rock itself was moved to Montezuma Street and thus became the first Whiskey Row saloon? This part of the story most likely stems from a transformation over time of a statement attributed to a Prescott old-timer and printed in a 1938 *Arizona Highways* article: "'The sight of water made the customers sick,' so they built the *rest of 'em* [italics added] up on Montezuma Street and called it Whiskey Row." Closeness to Granite Creek may have indeed been a liquor dealer's conundrum and the solution one street over. Most of the saloons were indeed later built on Montezuma Street.[20]

In 1865, the Quartz Rock was expanded. Another top quality billiard table was added. Although its history has been convoluted and, to some extent, mythologized, the true Quartz Rock story is vital to Whiskey Row history. For almost four years, the Quartz Rock was Prescott's leading tavern. It was the first saloon to receive a consistently significant amount of local media attention, the first to advertise on a week-to-week basis and the first go-to saloon in Prescott. Even if there were drunken men falling into or getting sick because of Granite Creek, the Quartz Rock stayed in one place and operated successfully on Granite Street for almost seven years. Did the Quartz Rock play a part in the birth and formation of Whiskey Row? Most certainly. It was the beginning of a block accommodating many saloons.[21]

Being Prescott's first get-together hub, the Quartz Rock hosted several colorful frontier stories. One undated but early story occurred when Prescott's primary concern was "Indian troubles." Lately, Indian signals—pseudo coyote yips and owl hoots—had been echoing back and forth throughout the forested mountains surrounding Fort Whipple and Prescott. The haunting sounds were thought to be coming from either Yavapai, Mohave or Tonto Apache. It was also observed that whenever scouting parties left Fort Whipple, smoke signals rose up from Prescott's circle of mountain summits. Yet numerous reconnaissance missions failed to locate any of the Indian lookouts until late one night when into the Quartz Rock walked a half-naked Sonoran boy claiming he'd escaped from the Tonto Apache after five years of captivity. To patrons there he described and pinpointed one especially essential lookout position. This information was relayed to the Fort Whipple commander. The next day, a unit of soldiers attacked the point, only to find, as usual, no one was there to attack. Yet the coyote howls and owl hoots ceased. The Quartz Rock info paid off.[22]

What was probably Prescott's first saloon murder occurred in the Quartz Rock on June 13, 1867, around six o'clock that evening. A well-known pioneer named William Murray was playing cards with several friends when in walked a younger man named George Crafts—apparently looking for trouble for its own sake—who "interfered" with the card game. Murray wasn't interested in suffering fools at that moment, so he threw his cards in Crafts's face. Crafts pulled his pistol. Murray was unarmed, but somehow snatched a revolver from the belt of the man standing next to him. Murray fired but missed Crafts, who returned fire. Murray pulled the trigger a second time, but the barrel of the revolver ruptured and exploded. Two of the three shots from Crafts's gun hit Murray, both near his heart. He died instantly. Crafts was immediately arrested and incarcerated at Fort Whipple. He had come from a well-to-do family in San Bernardino, California, who would "be shocked at his connection with this tragedy." Murray was buried in the Masonic Cemetery. According to the *Miner*, he left behind "an interesting wife and children."[23]

Almost three months later, on September 9, 1867, William Hardy sold the Quartz Rock to his first bartender, Andrew Moeller, for $6,600. For four more years, Moeller owned the Quart Rock before it suddenly went out of business.

FIRE!

Although the Juniper House had been taken by flames, and although not the first Prescott fire to be considered a conflagration, the one that occurred during the very early morning of March 26, 1871, was the first to directly effect the placement of saloons in Prescott and the most costly to date. Property loss was placed at over $15,000, more than $250,000 by today's standards.

In 1871, Prescott was of such a small size that Granite Street, only one street over from Montezuma, was considered west Prescott. There was no fire department at the time. The outcome of any emergency depended on the participation and efforts of nearby, willing citizenry. Around 2:00 a.m., flames were spotted coming out of the Quartz Rock. "Men dressed themselves hastily, started for the scene of the conflagration" and did what they could to quell the flames. Moeller, who'd been living in the Quartz Rock, had been fast asleep. He woke up surrounded by flames, quickly threw on some clothes and ran to safety on Granite Street. More than twenty barrels of his whiskey exploded, which guaranteed the complete destruction of Prescott's first legendary saloon. A larger catastrophe was flirted with when combustible items, including one hundred gallons of coal oil, ignited in the old store next door, now also owned by Moeller. The fire then roared north to the Pioneer Stable, which housed $300 worth of hay and grain, adding more fuel to the fire. There was great concern the fire would spread to the row of buildings on Montezuma and Gurley Streets. Dr. George Kendall proved the man of the hour, leading a group of men who'd run toward the danger: "Kendall accomplished more than any five men on the ground. He was everywhere, working, and directing others." Because of his and others' efforts, the fire was contained and prevented from establishing a domino effect throughout Prescott.[24]

The Quartz Rock wouldn't be rebuilt. However, almost three years prior, Moeller had jumped head first into a venture that was bigger and better. One of the buildings in danger of getting caught up in the March 26 fire was the one standing tall on the corner of Gurley and Montezuma Streets. It was Moeller's Diana Saloon, which had become the cornerstone for the emerging Whiskey Row.

THE CORNERSTONE OF WHISKEY ROW

Albert Osgood Noyes was one of early Prescott's most important residents. Like fellow pioneer George Barnard, Noyes, a New Englander, joined the thousands who traveled to the professed golden streams of California in 1849. He was also one of the many who in 1864, after not striking it rich in California, veered a touch east to test the mining opportunities being reported in the Central Arizona Highlands. After learning that a town would be quickly built around the newly established capital, Noyes and fellow pioneer George Lount recognized there was another exploitable natural resource even more abundant and accessible than ore and immediately in demand: trees, a limitless potential for making lumber. Here was a wide-open opportunity to win the financial prosperity Noyes initially sought in California. He would later write about Prescott to his sister, Olivia, "Certainly the chances of fortune and position are better here and there is no aristocracy."[25]

Lount and Noyes promptly traveled to San Francisco to purchase a sawmill. Toward the end of August and beginning of September 1864, portions of the mill arrived south of Prescott near a mountain topped with white onyx (often mistaken for quartz), Quartz Mountain. Soon, it was set up on the southern banks of Granite Creek, and Noyes and Lount were producing lumber at their Quartz Mountain Sawmill. This was big news. The dream that was Prescott could now more speedily become reality.[26]

Although he'd later also become a justice of the peace and probate judge, Noyes is best remembered as the man who owned and operated Prescott's first sawmill. It was once reported that he "has his law office at

[his] lumber lookout, east side of the plaza, where he whiles away his hours in measuring out lumber—and justice." During Prescott's first years, first with Lount and later George Curtis, Noyes held a monopoly over Prescott's lumber business. Noyes, Lount, Curtis and their timber were largely responsible for the expedient erection of many of the first buildings of Prescott. Contemporaneous newspaper reports and other recorded town histories, however, portray Noyes as the driving force behind the Quartz Mountain Sawmill.[27]

In July 1868, Noyes began circulating a rumor that a large building would soon grace the town. True to his word, he began construction on the southwest corner of Montezuma and Gurley Streets. As it was going up, locals marveled at the size of the frame. Noyes, often seen with his sleeves rolled up, measuring and sawing lumber, reported that it'd be a sixty- by twenty-eight-foot, two-story building. The first floor would be twelve and a half feet high, the second a half-foot higher. The upstairs would be reserved for civic organizations such as the Masons and Odd Fellows. The downstairs would be a first-class saloon.[28]

When Noyes first began building Prescott's soon-to-be grandest edifice, however, impediments immediately emerged. First, the weather wasn't always simpatico with Noyes's schedule and goals. Perhaps he wasn't yet familiar with the weather cycles of the Central Arizona Highlands—specifically, the monsoon temperament of its summers. During the early evening of Friday, August 14—shortly after construction began—a violent storm kicked up. It caused the normally tranquil Granite Creek to go "on a regular bender." Whole logs and ready-to-be-used lumber were carried away. Noyes's losses were considerable.[29]

The indomitable Noyes pushed on. Locals were amazed at how rapidly he and his crew were raising the structure. However, on Sunday, August 31, a little over two weeks after the Granite Creek debacle, a squall blew in from the northeast. Such was its strength that the walls of the partly roofed-and-shingled frame tumbled into an enormous pile. Noyes's losses amounted to about $1,000. He would again prove resolute. On Monday morning, Noyes and his crew assembled and, with pained expressions, began gathering the fallen lumber and were soon rebuilding. Again Prescottonians marveled when, by Friday, the structure was near the same degree of completion as it was before the winds knocked it down.[30]

Sometime in October, Noyes's prized edifice was finished. Locals predicted it would prove "an ornament to the town" and anticipated "some Jolly old times inside its glittering walls." Originally, the plan was to rent the downstairs to Cal Jackson. That was scrapped. Andrew Moeller anted up a hefty $8,500 and purchased Noyes's greatest creation in early November. After the losses incurred from the Granite Creek flashflood and the subsequent monsoon squall in August, Noyes decided to forego renting his big building. He accepted an offer by Moeller to buy it outright.[31]

Andrew Lucian "Doc" Moeller, like many other pioneer Prescottonians, transplanted himself from the East—in his case, Chambersburg, Pennsylvania. Once again, Moeller was one of many who headed west during the gold rush of 1849. After Abraham Lincoln made Arizona a United States territory in 1863, Moeller journeyed there and landed first in what would become Mohave County. After hearing better things were happening in the territory's central highlands, Moeller trekked southeast. As noted, in late 1864, he was hired as a bartender in William Hardy's Quartz Rock. Then Moeller's fortunes began to turn. As a property owner, he'd soon become nearly peerless in Prescott. In the 1870s, he owned at least twenty-seven lots throughout town and was bringing in $1,000 a month in rentals, over $22,000 by today's standards. His new saloon and meeting hall would become Moeller's most famous property. It can be fairly said that by becoming the proprietor of the legendary Quartz Rock and then establishing a grand, first-rate saloon on the corner of Montezuma and Gurley Streets, Andrew Moeller became the father of Whiskey Row. His new saloon, unnamed for almost a year, would become the mother of the Montezuma Street saloons.[32]

Soon, the idea spread that, because of this new "mammoth building," it was now possible for townsfolk to congregate in larger numbers in one place at the same time. Hence, a grand ball was planned. With Thanksgiving nearing, the timing was perfect. On November 21, a one-time advertisement was taken out in

Andrew Moeller owned two of early Whiskey Row's most important saloons: the Diana and the Quartz Rock. *Sharlot Hall Museum.*

THANKSGIVING BALL
AND SUPPER.

Having leased the MONTEZUMA HOTEL, we, the undersigned propose to inaugurate the event by giving a Grand Ball and Supper, in

Moeller's New Building,
On Thursday Evening, November 26, 1868.

FLOOR MANAGERS—Dr. Geo. D. Kendall, and N. P. Pierce.

The best Musicians in the country have been engaged.

Tickets, including Supper, which will be served at the Montezuma, Ten Dollars, currency.

WM. SILVERTHORN,
JOSEPH TODD.

Prescott, Arizona, Nov. 21, 1868.

Andrew Moeller's new building hosted Prescott's first big ball. *Sharlot Hall Museum.*

the *Miner*, announcing a "THANKSGIVING BALL AND SUPPER." The *Miner* made a separate report promising this event would "be the biggest and best blowout ever given in the Territory." Further piquing the public's already aroused curiosity was that it would be held in Moeller's new building. "The hall is the finest and largest in Arizona" the *Miner* ad claimed. Perhaps this is why the organizers felt justified to charge an outrageous ten dollars for the affair, outrageous because a complete meal could be bought for fifty cents or less anywhere else in town. Of course, there'd be more. Musicians, reputedly the best the region had to offer, had been hired to play the whole night long.[33]

When Thanksgiving evening rolled around, the pristinely floored room was packed wall-to-wall with a fair amount of ladies and a disproportionate number of men who had come to dance the night away, which they did, some until dawn. Two *Miner* reporters attended with the excuse of gathering information to make a report. With difficulty, they waded across the room of dancers to a corner. They wanted a headcount of the ladies present and found a spot they thought would "keep their corns from being trampled upon." Cornered with them was an older man, who was asked if he knew how many of the fairer sex were present. He was unable to answer. The object of his hoped-for affections was otherwise occupied, "tripping the light fantastic" with another, and he was too filled with the "green monster" to respond.

The *Miner* boys went about counting the ladies themselves and came up with forty, not counting the married ones, "for they have no hearts to give away." The other gender? Four times more, making for the sad sight of men of all ages waiting on the sidelines hoping for a chance to dance with a lovely lady. The night ended for the reporters after an encounter with an auburn-haired girl, one of the few of her sex waiting for a dance. After her request to dance was rejected—"we muttered something about awkwardness and told her that to please her we would do anything but dance, even marry you sooner than dance with you"—the gentlemen were bade in no uncertain terms to go home, which they did. But they'd seen enough to discern that the ball had been a fabulous success.[34]

As memorable as the Thanksgiving ball was, it wasn't the grand opening of Moeller's new drinking and billiard saloon. That occurred eight days later on December 5. Immediately, the gambling and billiard tables were top draws, as were, of course, the extensive choice of libations. Using his experience as bartender and proprietor of the Quartz Rock, Moeller made his "new billiard and drinking saloon [the] best finished and furnished in the Territory." This was the opinion of many who attended the Diana's opening night. Moeller had brought over from the Quartz Rock the man with whom he'd shared original bartending duties in that pioneering bar, Joe Crane. With Bill Linn, "the two amiable bartenders had all they could do to keep the thirsty crowd moistened" during the glorious affair. The second story became known as "Moeller's Hall" and was used for meetings of civic organizations, as planned.[35]

The name of Moeller's saloon wasn't yet known to the public. It was, however, so dominantly successful that Moeller initially felt no need to advertise. Being abundantly peopled meant there would be an abundance of good times and festive occasions, as predicted. It also guaranteed trouble. In the late 1860s, pioneer Prescottonians weren't generally carrying meek souls around with them. They were normally men of rugged bravado possessing risk-taking, competitive dispositions. A few in that barrel were just bad men. When animated by their favorite spirits, a seemingly typical night could turn sour.

WHISKEY ROW'S FIRST "BLOODIEST NIGHT"

Around four o'clock in the morning of September 20, 1869, two men were shot dead and one seriously wounded in Moeller's saloon. The September 25 *Miner* report of this tragic incident called it "the bloodiest in the annals of this town." It was also the first time the name of Moeller's billiard and drinking establishment appeared in print: the Diana Saloon. The killed and wounded men were active soldiers from Fort Whipple. Sergeant Patrick McGovern of the Eighth Cavalry had been shot dead, as had Private Thomas Donahue of the Twelfth Infantry. Private George Nunes, also of the Twelfth Infantry, was the recipient of a knife wound. How and why the fight started wasn't disclosed, but whiskey was in the thick of it.

The accused? There were also three. Private Harry Langham, still active with the Twelfth Infantry, and two discharged soldiers, Joseph Johnson and William Collins. Only Langham, who stabbed Nunes and was suspected of killing Donahue, was caught and arrested that morning. Eyewitnesses claimed that Johnson shot McGovern. Collins was thought to have abetted Johnson. Both fled from the Diana and scurried south. Sergeant McGovern's unit, the Eighth Cavalry, immediately began pursuing the fugitives, led by Indian war veteran Lieutenant McCleave. The *Miner* didn't mince words when wishing for the outcome: "it is the prayer of this entire community that they will be killed or captured."[36]

The military "posse" followed a trail that led south through the Bradshaw Mountains and then the McDowells. The Eighth Cavalry resupplied at Fort McDowell, where they also acquired some Pima Indian scouts. With their help, McCleave and his men moved past the Salt River Valley. The trail became hot some fifty miles below in the Sacaton Mountains. In the hills above the Little Gila River and near the Sacaton Station, a former stopping point along the Butterfield Overland Mail Route, Johnson and Collins were trapped and captured on October 8. McCleave unhesitatingly gave credit to

The Diana Saloon on the corner of Montezuma and Gurley Streets hosted both happy and terrible times for fifteen years. *Sharlot Hall Museum.*

the Pima scouts. On October 14, a Lieutenant Kane and his troops brought the prisoners to Yavapai County sheriff John Taylor, who lodged them in jail to await a grand jury trial. A week later, a party of Pima Indians showed up in Prescott. Their intentions? To get what they deserved: payment for their part in capturing Johnson and Collins.[37]

The story didn't end there. The trial of Joseph Johnson and William Collins was set for the first week of May 1870. On Tuesday night, April 26, Sheriff John Taylor, before going home, made sure his prisoners were securely locked up. Apparently, however, the jailhouse had no night guard. Johnson and Collins were sharing a cell, which was primarily wooden. From friends on the outside, they'd somehow obtained an auger and saw, which they hid. When Wednesday morning rolled around and Sheriff Taylor made his customary visit to the jails, he found a sizable hole in the rear wall of Johnson and Collins's cell. They had sawed and drilled a section out of a large log that formed part of the wall, crawled through it and escaped with an ease that troubled locals. It was the first jailbreak in Prescott history. Taylor immediately advertised a $300 reward for the six foot, black-eyed Johnson and $200 for the shorter, blue-eyed, light-skinned Collins. They were never caught.

In spite of this tragedy, the Diana was still considered the best saloon in the territory. It was a sight to behold, "now gorgeous with chaste pictures, beautiful paper, nice paint, fantastic chandeliers, billiard tables, and such." Joe Crane was still bartending and assisting in other ways. The "whole souled" Joe, it was said, could make someone happy even happier, and "we know of no better place to drink than at the bar of the Diana." Later in the 1870s, Crane would take over proprietorship of the Diana.[38]

Almost three years after the Diana was opened, the Quartz Rock burned down. Nevertheless, the first bracket of Whiskey Row's genealogy had taken shape, and its cornerstone was firmly established. The next matriarch in the row's family would be born in 1874: the Cabinet Saloon. However, in 1868—after the territorial capital had moved to Tucson—the survival of Prescott was an unanswered question. Lawless towns in the Old West later became the breeding grounds for thrilling reading, movies and television shows. But for those actually living there, fear was the prevalent emotion and lawlessness a state to be conquered. So it was four years into the life of Prescott.

Chapter 3

Law and Order, and Lawlessness, Along the Emergent Whiskey Row

Saloons "till you can't rest" where they kill a man at least once a week. There was only one man killed at Prescott during my sojourn.
—Arizona Territory pioneer Sylvester Mowry, describing Prescott in 1871 during a short visit[39]

After the Diana Saloon slayings of September 20, 1869, violent crimes became more commonplace along "the row." Most were fueled by whiskey, and most took place in a saloon, or at least started in one. In March 1869, after two respected men came "under the influence of the abominable beverage" and acted in a manner that endangered themselves and everyone around them—in a way they wouldn't have behaved had they not been drinking—it was wished by some locals that "every drop of whisky on the continent was in Africa or China." In the late autumn of that year, Sheriff Taylor was strolling down Montezuma Street when a shot resounded and a bullet passed through the sheriff's coat sleeve. At the time, the shooter was unknown. That changed on Tuesday evening, December 7. Taylor was summoned to an undisclosed Whiskey Row saloon because a soldier named Pegan had drank too much "punching whiskey" and was looking for a fight. Taylor was able to arrest him, but on the way to jail, Pegan's tongue became as loose as his fists had been clenched. He bragged to Taylor that it was he who'd taken the potshot at him a few days prior and come "within an ace of making himself a murderer." Yet, to the dismay of those who knew about the bullet Pegan intended for their sheriff, he was fined only fifty dollars for drunken behavior.[40]

This was only a warm up for another night of horror at the Diana.

A Second Bloody Night at the Diana

A notorious desperado, Hiram Lightner, was in Prescott in the early summer of 1870. He decided to visit its most popular attraction, the Diana. On Wednesday night, June 29, he was engaged in a card game with native Missourian Sion Bradley, a forty-something professional gambler who had a drinking problem. In spite of this, Bradley also had a reputation for being an honorable man and, ironically, "the best pistol shot on the Pacific Coast." At some point, the game got out of control. Lightner and Bradley began arguing. When Lightner reached his boiling point, he pulled a pistol and began shooting at Bradley. Four shots left his gun—plenty to show that murder was his intent. Bradley, the noted pistoleer, was unarmed for a change, intoxicated and completely defenseless. One bullet went astray, but three struck Lightner's target. One particularly egregious bullet hit him in the groin and subsequently passed through his bladder. Drs. George Kendall and James McCandless were called to the scene. A makeshift operating room was set up in the Diana. They worked together to successfully extract the bullets, but Bradley remained in critical condition.

Lightner attacked Bradley so suddenly that no one present was able to gather his wits quickly enough to do anything about it. The assailant escaped. A physical description was published: "Lightner is about 5 feet 10 inches in height, of sandy complexion; wore Burnsides whiskers; had on a chequered shirt and pants made of material resembling corduroy. He is a very bad man." Doctors fought hard to save Bradley. He lingered for six days before finally succumbing in the very early morning of July 5. Bradley's death was used as a cautionary tale in the fight against the two most despised vices in Prescott: "His fate should be a warning to other men who are following the same course of life—gambling and drinking— for, sooner or later, it will lead them into trouble." Hiram Lightner turned himself in to Sheriff Taylor on Independence Day, the day before Bradley passed away.[41]

A SUNDAY CHURCH SERVICE TO REMEMBER ACROSS FROM WHISKEY ROW

A popular publication in the 1860–70s was *Harper's New Monthly Magazine* out of New York City. It featured a widely read column called "Editors Drawer," which imparted, often with hyperbole and creative dialogue, colorful nonfiction stories. Three months after Sion Bradley was murdered in the Diana, a Sunday church service was held at 5:00 p.m. on October 2, 1870, in the Plaza directly across from the saloons on Montezuma Street. An incident therein would've made good copy for the "drawer," no exaggerations required. Leading the service were two missionaries, Miss Garrison and Mrs. Cedarholm, both of whom were keen on reforming topers. A large crowd composed solely of men—some of whom hadn't been completely abstemious during the day—gathered to listen to the ladies. A handful were soused and "not so heavenly in character." Yet they listened intently when Miss Garrison sang songs, offered prayers and instruction and while Mrs. Cedarholm served up "a very earnest, sensible exhortation."

The fun began when the program was turned back over to Miss Garrison. She preached against the evils of alcoholic admixtures and made the claim that "the Bible said that no drunkards could enter the kingdom of heaven." Two of the more drunk fellows thought "Miss G." was referring specifically to them. The first responded loud enough for everyone to hear, "Well, we don't want to, Hell is all we claim." The undaunted missionary went on to admonish those there to turn from the error of their ways and that "Jesus Christ says his blood cleanseth from all sin." The second muddle-minded man reacted with, "Eh? What? How? Did [he] say that? G—d d—n him, I'll make him take it back." This, of course, caused an uncomfortable stir among the crowd. One wise and benignant member of the audience suggested that the two intoxicated interjectors return to the saloons, a suggestion to which they gladly agreed. The pair wobbled away, and the resolute Miss Garrison "went on, as though nothing had happened."[42]

The ladies' fire and brimstone had no effect on Whiskey Row, although every now and then a soaker would pledge "to never get drunk again." The proliferation of gambling and drinking along Whiskey Row continued. In fact, Mrs. Cedarholm fell out of favor with Prescottonians in 1871. She had traveled to San Francisco to beg the more civilized people there to provide funds for building a church in church-less Prescott. In doing so, she felt it necessary to "belittle the people of Prescott." Mrs. Cedarholm spoke of their whiskey and gambling vices and asserted they were incapable of raising

"Without me ye can do nothing."—*John* 15, 5.

TOTAL ABSTINENCE PLEDGE.

I solemnly promise, by the grace of God, that I will Abstain from the use of all Intoxicating Drinks as a Beverage; that I will neither make, buy, sell, or offer such to any person, and will try to induce others to do the same.

(*Signed in duplicate.*)...

Witness,...

(*Date,*)..

"I can do all things through Christ which strengtheneth me."—*Phil.* 4, 13.

"Help thou my infirmities."

"My Grace is sufficient."

Missionaries sometimes raided Whiskey Row saloons in an attempt to get whiskey drinkers to sign an abstinence pledge like the one shown above. *Nancy Burgess.*

a church on their own. After returning to Prescott, she asked to speak at a local religious gathering. She was rejected. Her characterization of Prescott to Californians wasn't appreciated. Yet many Prescottonians didn't completely disagree with missionary Cedarholm; they knew their town was heading dangerously toward anarchy if not possible extinction. Something had to be done.[43]

The years 1869 and '70 found Prescott undergoing some introspection and self-evaluation: "There is no use disguising the fact that Prescott is fast becoming a disorderly town, and unless something be speedily done to check the desperados who occasionally visit us, we might as well cease talking about law," read the *Miner* of October 22, 1870. Earlier that year, it was noted, "Indulgence in gambling, drinking, and other vices has been nearly as hard upon our people and country. But we have gone off our trail, and must now return." It was descried that their young village had more saloons and gambling tables than even the bigger towns in California. The pith of Prescott, in their minds, was being poisoned: "We know our people would be better off were there no saloons in the Territory." Then there was the issue of a blinding absence of religion in Prescott, as preached by missionaries Garrison and Cedarholm. In late 1870, some were concerned that "while the nice, attractive town is crowded with saloons it strikes the visitor's eyes that there is no church and not much Christian life and association." Visiting preachers tried to infiltrate Prescott's soul, putting forth the gospel of Jesus Christ but equating it with the gospel of anti-saloon and anti-whiskey sentiments.[44]

"Whiskey Row" hadn't yet fully earned its famous moniker in the late 1860s and early 1870s, but it was well on its way. In a town becoming too fond of whiskey, most of the trouble, as might be imagined, occurred at night or early morning. The crisis was recognized as far back as December 1869, when the local section of the *Miner* published a plea: "WATCHMAN NEEDED," followed by: "Our once quiet village is getting to be a regular Pandemonium. Drunken men quarrel, fight, and shoot. Let us have a night watchman or two, who will muzzle the men."[45]

NIGHT WATCHMAN WILLIAM JENNINGS

An effective night watchman—not a position by appointment or election but one paid for by a pool of Prescott businessmen—didn't surface until sometime before 1871. Prescott has had its share of legendary lawmen. Its first effective peace officer was William Jennings, a transplanted Englishman who wasn't a marshal, sheriff or chief of police but its original night watchman. By 1872, he'd established a rock-solid reputation of sustained dependability. After one shooting incident on Granite Street, it was reported, "Jennings was on hand, *as usual*, [italics added] and put a stop to it."

WILLIAM JENNINGS,
NIGHT WATCHMAN.
Attends to Calls at all Hours.

The night watchman posted a "business card" in the *Miner* because it was not a position by appointment or election; it was voluntary and paid for by a pool of Prescott businessmen. *Sharlot Hall Museum.*

Granite Street was often the source of early trouble in Prescott. Another major incident occurred on that thoroughfare in March 1873. Around eleven o'clock one evening, the ever-vigilant Jennings, the one-man police force, heard a shot. He immediately moved toward the sound, believing it had come from a house of ill repute on Granite Street. Upon arriving, he found some soldiers trying to bust through the bordello windows. The seemingly fearless Jennings ordered them to stop. They did not. So Jennings, à la Wyatt Earp, made an example of one of the soldiers by pistol-whipping him into submission. He then used a lit match like a flashlight, by means of which he discovered that a soldier had been shot and was clearly in critical condition. Jennings somehow obtained medical help, which was given in the gunman's house. The wounded soldier was conveyed by wagon to Fort Whipple. The shooter was a former cook at Fort Whipple who'd made several enemies there. He was later found and arrested. The friends of the soldier were endeavoring to kill the shooter that evening, and they surely would have, had Jennings not stepped in.[46]

Law enforcement by pistol butt was employed again in the fall of 1873, after a man, again on Granite Street, had assaulted a woman with a hatchet. Jennings first shot the man through the hand holding the hatchet, disarming him. He then used the butt of his pistol to pacify the assailant with a swift blow to his nose. Prescottonians felt safer with Jennings roaming the village streets at night. The *Miner* expressed the town's general feeling about him: "Prescott brags on her nightwatchman, Mr. Wm. Jennings, who knows so well how to preserve the peace and watch over the lives and property of his sleeping brothers and sisters."[47]

William Jennings was the hero of Prescott in the early and mid-1870s, but his heroics would be overshadowed in 1877 by a sudden change of behavior. His life would take a drastic turn, as would the position of night watchman. His downfall would be more rapid than his ascension. All heroes have an Achilles' heel, and Jennings was no exception. When equipped with an adequate amount of financing, he'd inveterately be found "bucking the tiger" at a faro table in a Whiskey Row saloon. In fact, after Jennings had taken the night watchman job, he soon resigned but then was either persuaded to retake the responsibility, or he came to his senses. An early 1871 *Miner* report barked that Jennings had "quit in disgust, because he could not make a fortune by watching and bucking the tiger."[48]

Faro was exactly what he was playing in the early morning of November 23, 1877, in a Montezuma Street saloon—probably the Cabinet Saloon. What transpired toward the end of his faro games that morning is unknown, but at some point, something went amiss. After leaving the saloon, Jennings took a walk down a Prescott street with village marshal Frank Murray. Suddenly, charging toward Jennings came the faro dealer, Larry Tullock. Tullock began to chastise Jennings so vehemently for some perceived offense that Murray seized, cuffed and arrested him. Then the unthinkable happened. Murray was walking the faro dealer to jail when Jennings promptly drew his knife and lunged at Tullock, intending to stab him in the stomach. Murray swung and literally lifted Tullock away, but Jennings's follow-through landed his knife deep into one of Tullock's thighs.

This changed everything. Tullock was sent to get medical help; Jennings was arrested and immediately relieved from night watchman duties. For several years after, that challenging position proved difficult to keep filled. Even Virgil Earp gave the job a shot but resigned after a short stint. In January 1878, Jennings was sentenced to six months of prison. While incarcerated, he began showing signs of mental disturbance, seeing spirits and hearing voices. When released, however, the irrepressible Jennings didn't stay out of the news for long. He headed for the Hassayampa District and soon discovered that his knack for ore-hunting was even greater than his exceptional talent for Wild West law enforcement.[49]

A second Achilles' heel soon surfaced, however: whiskey. In early April 1879, after picking up supplies at the Bashford general store, Jennings left with the intention of returning to his mines but "was detained at several points" along Whiskey Row. Nightfall arrived, and an inebriated Jennings finally guided his two burros south down Montezuma Street. A mile or two from town, he passed out in the middle of the road. The next morning, he discovered that while his burros were still with him, he'd been robbed of everything else. The *Miner* joked that perhaps the robbers had "administered chloroform or some other stupefying drug."[50]

Yet, by early July, it was happily reported that Jennings was a true "bonanza king"; his operations were so successful that he was described as having "mineral in front of him and mineral in the rear of him." Time after time, the *Miner* gave reports akin to the following: "Jennings is in from his Hassayampa bonanzas, which are numerous and rich." Some predicted that if his luck continued, he would become the richest man in the territory.[51]

Jennings, however, showed signs of further mental illness, surfacing most visibly in September 1882. The *Prescott Courier* (referred to hereafter as the *Courier*) reported that he was "now a little 'off' in his mind," describing him as "the insane man from the Hassayampa." Paranoia caused him to believe enemies were trying to poison him, so when one neighbor visited Jennings's well for water, he tried to shoot him. Jennings was soon arrested and, within a week, carted off to the insane asylum in Stockton, California.[52]

Jennings didn't return to his mines until sometime in 1884, but when he did, his bonanza ways continued for another eight years. As time went by, the living legend became more reclusive. So when he hadn't been seen in Prescott for two weeks during the second half of September 1892, there was no immediate concern. His neighbors, however, became worried and decided to pay him a visit. One of them later traveled into town and reported that he'd seen a body at the bottom of a mine. His friend, Dan Hatz, rode out and found Jennings sitting upright and dead on the mine's deepest bench, 110 feet below. Thus ended the life of William Jennings, one of Prescott's first heroes who became "the well-known and eccentric miner of the Hassayampa."[53]

While a semblance of law and order was being restored, Whiskey Row was afforded an opportunity to grow. In 1874, when Jennings was still serving as the row's night watchman, it took the next step in its evolution. A new saloon arose that would prove most influential along the pre–Great Fire Whiskey Row. Its specter still dwells there today.

Chapter 4
The "Cabinet"

The Heartbeat of Early Whiskey Row

Today, Whiskey Row's showpiece is the magnificent Palace Restaurant and Saloon, which in 2014 was listed by *USA Today* as one of "The Ten Best Bars That Serve Up History." But in the pre–Great Fire years of Whiskey Row, it was the Cabinet Saloon that essentially served as its heartbeat for nearly a quarter of a century. It still does. Although it requires a bit of scholarly time and tracing, it's not difficult to establish, with perfect solidity, that the "Cabinet" was the true first version of the Palace and its origination point.

The Cabinet was co-founded and driven to success by one of early Prescott's most colorful characters and innovative entrepreneurs, Daniel Conner "D.C" Thorne. According to his son, Daniel Thorne Jr., "My father had the distinction of opening in 1868 the famous Palace Bar, where the present Palace now stands on Whiskey Row (Montezuma Street)." This statement can be divided into three parts: two parts false and one part true. The part that is true, however, carries more weight than both falsehoods.[54]

Although Dan Thorne would actually have proprietorship of the pre–Great Fire Palace Saloon between 1887 and 1891, he did not inaugurate it, at least in the sense of using the moniker "Palace." Hence, in a very superficial sense, Thorne Jr.'s statement is false. However, as just stated, Thorne was the founder of the Cabinet Saloon. More than half of what would become the rebuilt post–Great Fire Palace Saloon does indeed rest where, at one time or another, Thorne's Cabinet and its associated businesses stood from 1874 (not 1868, which is the second falsehood) to 1900; the Cabinet was situated on lot 19, until it burned down in 1883, and then on lot 21 after it was rebuilt. It stayed there until the Great Fire of 1900. Lot 20, 120 Montezuma Street was often used for businesses associated with the Cabinet and later by the Palace after it was moved from Goodwin Street to Montezuma Street in 1884. Sometimes the Cabinet and Palace used lot 20 simultaneously by dividing it into two sections, front and rear. After 1901, the Palace stood proudly on lots 19, 20 and 21. Today, the Palace's saloon section and most of the dining area are situated on lot 20 and the rest on the back halves of lots 19 and 21.

More significantly, the truth regarding the Palace's origins can be best distilled by starting with the following fact: when the Palace and Cabinet saloons were both destroyed in the Great Fire of 1900, instead of rebuilding separately, Robert Brow of the Palace and Ben Belcher and Barney Smith of the Cabinet decided, rather than continue to compete against one another, to merge their institutions. In the end, the two saloons' histories cannot be separated. Illuminating this fact, the final product was not initially going to be called the Palace or the Cabinet. On the back of the original blueprint for the Brow, Belcher and Smith merger venture, a revealing change was made. The original agreement between that illustrious troika—perhaps as a compromise—was to call their risen-from-flames, melded experiment the "National Saloon," and it was labeled as such on the blueprint. However, sometime during the process, the word "National" was scribbled out. Inked in over the top was the replacement name: "Palace." At some point, likely after the blueprints' directions were being physically applied and the end result could be visualized, the name "Palace" became more fitting, and thus it was named. But make no mistake—although its name was left behind, the new palatial edifice was just as much an expansion of the Cabinet as it was the pre–Great Fire Palace.[55]

Although technically the originator of the Cabinet Saloon, D.C. Thorne, more than any other, merits the distinction of being christened the founder of the famed Palace Saloon, to which so many stories and legends have

Originally, when the Palace Saloon was being rebuilt in 1900–01, it was going to be called the National Saloon. *Sharlot Hall Museum.*

been attributed. Names are superficial things. They can be erased as easily as a pencil mark, but the entity behind the name remains. The entity in this case was the Palace Saloon. It all began with the relentless Thorne. He lived for almost thirteen more years after the Great Fire of 1900. In 1901, if Thorne had stood with his family in front of the new and grandest saloon in the Southwest, the new Palace Saloon, and boasted, "This all started with me; I founded this place in 1874," he would not have been lying. The Palace's lineage zigzags here and there but eventually leads straight to Thorne's Cabinet Saloon of 1874.

What began as the Cabinet in 1874 is now the Palace Restaurant and Saloon, with the Jersey Lilly Saloon upstairs. *Norman Fisk.*

No one had more influence on the early history of Whiskey Row than D. C. Thorne. His is truly a Whiskey Row legacy story.

Dynamic Dan Thorne

Daniel Conner Thorne was one of early Prescott's most enduringly successful men. He was a man with a magic touch and voracious lust for life around whom activity and stories swirled. By now it seems redundant, but Thorne, a native New Yorker, was one of the thousands lured to the West after news of the discovery of gold in California reached the East. Equally repetitive, the personal result was unsatisfactory. There were pit stops along the way, but he eventually moved to Prescott in 1867 when in his late thirties. The Bradshaw and Sierra Prieta Mountains surrounding Prescott were the latest "Sutter Creek," and Thorne was still looking for his fortune. He quickly

Daniel Conner Thorne, shown on the right here with Robert Brow and Charlie Gray, influenced Whiskey Row history more than any other person. *Sharlot Hall Museum.*

invested in several nearby mines. The Central Arizona Highlands proved what California and Sutter Creek couldn't, for Thorne was soon on his way to realizing his dreams.[56]

The first time Thorne appeared in the *Miner* was on January 1, 1870, after he equaled the future sheriff of Cochise County of Tombstone infamy, Johnny Behan, in a pigeon-shooting contest held on Christmas day on the Plaza. Soon after this, he made a trip east to play a more serious game. He had earlier boasted to his cronies that he was going there to "commit matrimony." His friends laughed in disbelief because, after all, he had no one in mind with whom to do such a thing. That didn't stop Thorne. At some point during his time away, he met a New Jersey girl, Mary Wilson. On February 28, he married her. By June, they were back in Prescott and having a $2,000 house built on North Montezuma Street. Thorne's friends were learning to take him at his word.[57]

Thorne began seeing profits from his mining ventures in the early 1870s. Now he was able to delve into other business opportunities, which seemed unlimited in 1870s Prescott. At some point in 1874, Thorne, along with William Hutchinson, rented the building sitting on lot 19, 118 Montezuma Street, and opened a saloon. It featured a cabinet seen immediately after walking through the saloon's doors that showcased an extensive collection of exceptional ore specimens mined from the Bradshaws and Sierra Prieta. Hence, at least in part, the name "Cabinet," a clever invitation to miners, the area's most employed group. By July, the "new resort"—which also featured a popular Chinese chophouse in the rear—was already attracting large crowds. D.C. Thorne the mining man would remain active, but Thorne the saloon man was born. It was a label by which he would become a household name in Prescott for decades. Now the Diana had legitimate competition, and the history of Whiskey Row suddenly escalated to another level.[58]

Three years into the Cabinet's existence, Thorne found himself in the middle of a real-life Wild West situation that would symbolize the way he lived. To him, it was just another story and the way of the frontier.

FAMOUS HIGHWAYMAN "BRAZEN BILL" BRAZELTON MEETS THE CABINET SALOON'S D.C. THORNE

On Thursday morning at 6:00 a.m., September 27, 1877, a California-bound stagecoach left Prescott. D.C. Thorne was aboard. According to Thorne family history, he requested and was permitted to ride shotgun alongside the stagecoach driver because, after all, there was no better seat for viewing the countryside. An event involving Thorne—and later the Cabinet—and an infamous highwayman known as "Brazen Bill" Brazelton would occur that day. Brazen Bill, who worked solo, was considered by some to be the most successful stage robber of his time.

Inside the coach was the founder of the renowned Peck Mine, Ed Peck, along with his wife, children and his aged mother and father. Riding with the Pecks was Gus Ellis. The coach was transporting several mailbags, a Wells Fargo express box within which was a package of gold dust and bars valued at $1,300, another containing small gold bars worth $470 and two large gold ingots worth $4,000. Most of the gold belonged to Peck, who also had a large sum of money on his person.

The road to California passed through Wickenburg. In between Prescott and Wickenburg was a stop called Antelope Station, which was also a mini-boomtown due to nearby gold discoveries. Eight miles south was where passenger Thorne would find himself in a life-or-death situation. When the stagecoach dropped down from a mesa and into a wash, there waiting with a shotgun was Brazelton, who was known for masking his face with white or black kerchiefs. Brazen Bill ordered the driver to get down and hold the horses by the bits and for Thorne to throw down the express box. Keeping his shotgun trained on Thorne, his next command was for the saloon man to step slowly off the coach. Brazelton threw Thorne an axe to smash open the box. After Thorne handed its contents to the highwayman, Brazen Bill then ordered Ellis, still inside the stagecoach with the Pecks, to throw out the mailbags. They, too, were cut open by Thorne and their insides given to Brazelton.

Winds were gusting this day. One kicked up at just the right—or wrong—time. According to Thorne, this blast temporarily dislodged Brazen Bill's mask, just enough for Thorne to get a look at the thief before he quickly slipped the kerchief back in place. Thorne had seen the criminal's face, which suddenly made him disposable, and Brazen Bill said as much. Before carrying out this threat, Bill asked the driver if the horses would "stand fire" at the crack of his gun. The driver said he thought they would but mentioned that women and children were inside the coach. This apparently was the reason Bill spared Thorne's life. The thief then jumped atop his horse and fled with his loot. Inexplicably, Ed Peck's gold ingots were left behind, and he was never searched for the money he was holding.

Thorne never provided a description of the robber to authorities, even after encountering Brazen Bill again shortly after the robbery. The following episode is one of several attributed to occurring in the Palace when in fact it happened in the Cabinet. One day, Thorne was standing at the end of his bar and facing the Cabinet's swinging doors when in walked none other than Brazen Bill. The two had a quick stare-down. Both recognized each other. Bill immediately about-faced, and they never saw each other again. Thorne was disappointed that the highwayman didn't stay longer. The story he shared with his family was that he was so grateful that Brazen Bill spared his life and, in his words, "didn't even rob me; I would have showed him the time of his life and the drinks would

"Big Nose Kate," who went by many names and accompanied Doc Holliday during his famous winning streak on Whiskey Row in 1880, is buried in the Arizona Pioneer Home Cemetery in Prescott. *Norman Fisk.*

have been on the house." Such was the fleeting and only known connection Brazen Bill would have with Whiskey Row.[59]

When Brazen Bill Brazelton walked into the Cabinet Saloon that day, he may've noticed an unusual something else. Thorne had a mascot: a cinnamon-colored bear cub. The local joke was that Thorne had found the ultimate bouncer. If somebody in the saloon became belligerent, "the young bruin [would] be turned loose, and if not able to command the peace will at least be able to 'clean out' the crowd."[60]

The Cabinet Saloon's history, however, had just begun. Of all the pre–Great Fire saloons, it would become the most storied, although not necessarily in written or even oral history. When Doc Holliday had his famous winning streak on Whiskey Row with his mistress "Big Nose Kate" at his side in 1880, it was most likely in the Cabinet, the chief gambling hall in Prescott. Before his friends Wyatt and Virgil Earp departed Prescott for Tombstone and everlasting fame, Doc, not wanting to slap Lady Luck in the face, stayed for an extra three months as a "sporting man" on Whiskey Row.

The Cabinet would yield a history and legacy that is arguably unmatched in the American Southwest's frontier saloon history. But while the Cabinet was achieving prominence, Whiskey Row's history would take some intriguing turns.

LAWLESSNESS RETURNS

Nightwatchman William Jennings had rendered an improvement in law and order on Whiskey Row. When he was removed from his position in 1877, out-of-control lawlessness made a short return. The issue by then had shifted from the prohibition of whiskey and toward the promotion of quality whiskey. Phil Kearney, who'd been Fort Whipple's first and "best telegrapher that ever handled a key in this latitude," switched occupations and decided to become Prescott's missionary proselytizing "a purer spirit of whisky." He opened a saloon bearing his name and a sample room and introduced Prescott to J.H. Cutter No. 1 Bourbon Whisky, distilled in Kentucky and sold from San Francisco. Quoting Shakespeare, Kearney told Prescottonians that if they wanted to "'put an enemy in their heads to steal away their brains,' they shall have an opportunity to take it from the fountain head." There would be a converse reformation. No more "Jersey Lightning" or "Blue Ruin" in this renaissance. Thus was initiated a bit of competition to provide quality liquors in Prescott, even to the point of sacrificing a bit of profit. Was this a good thing?[61]

Sometimes whiskey was enjoyed outside in the front of Whiskey Row saloons. On June 27, 1877, two men unknown to each other were doing just that in front of the Cabinet. One, James Stone—clearly absent of any aristocratic comportment—noticed another, described only as a "gentleman," enjoying a chew of tobacco. Stone asked for a taste. The gentleman complied by giving Stone a plug of "Old Navy" tobacco. Stone took it, gave it a sniff and took this provision as a personal affront. He vehemently explained that he preferred the sweeter, more nectarous "Ida May" chew. Not only that, Stone complained, but Old Navy was akin to bovine manure and its supplier no better. That was the final straw. The gentleman suddenly became less gentle and tackled Stone to the ground. A scuffle ensued, and the two wound up two doors down in front of the Nugget Saloon. Stone had been "whipped." When village marshal Frank Murray arrived on the scene, he let the gentleman go but arrested Stone. It wasn't wise to insult a man's tobacco products on Whiskey Row.[62]

In late 1877, without an effective night watchman in place, the elected position of village marshal became even more important in Prescott. Murray was allowed to appoint a deputy village marshal. In September, he chose Joe Price to fulfill that role. On the same day he was appointed, Murray assigned him the night watch. Just a few hours into that shift, he heard shots coming from Granite Street. Price hurried toward the commotion. He found a mule packer from Fort Whipple, Thomas Bennett, having "a jamboree, and making it lively for the boys at the New Bit Saloon." Price gained control of Bennett, wrestled his Smith & Wesson .45-caliber pistol from him and arrested him. However, he failed to take into account that the gun was still cocked. Price bumped his finger against the trigger. Luckily, the gun was pointed downward. The bullet struck the big bone at the top of Price's foot, penetrating to the instep and out the sole of his boot. Needless to say, Price's career was put on hold but not due to a lack of bravery. It could've been worse, but it was thought Price would be out of commission for several months.[63]

Price proved a quick healer. Sometime before December, he was back on the streets. Price would make a name for himself that month after taking on Whiskey Row's saloon-hopping bully, Big Jim Donigan. As feared as he was, he was also looked upon as a marvel by the locals: "Big Jim Donigan seems to have the faculty of getting shot oftener than anyone, but he can walk away with more lead in him than any ordinary mortal." Around Christmas,

Donigan got into another scrape in an undisclosed saloon, to which Price was summoned. Donigan became so threatening that Price felt it necessary to aim his gun at his head. After firing multiple times, one shot finally connected. A bullet passed through one cheek, then through his mouth before lodging into the opposite jawbone. In the process, one of Donigan's teeth sliced in half, which he "promptly spit out as being no longer useful." Dr. Warren Day—a notorious polygamist but good doctor—extracted the bullet from Donigan's jaw. There was no need for anesthesia. The copious amount of whiskey he'd drank before the shooting proved the only numbing agent needed.[64]

A return to law and order was once more needed. It would come beginning in 1878 when Deputy Sheriff James Dodson began asserting his influence along Whiskey Row. His service would facilitate an era of prosperity led by the Diana, Cabinet and Palace saloons. Before marching into that time and continuing the histories of these establishments, a look at some of the saloons that accompanied them during the early growth of Whiskey Row is needed.

Chapter 5

The Montezuma, Jackson & Tompkins' and Keystone Saloons

Contributors to Whiskey Row's Growing Notoriety

After 1874, the Cabinet Saloon became Whiskey Row's domineering force. Yet one of its contemporaries, the Montezuma Saloon, stretched back to the days of the Quartz Rock, with which it went head to head in a popularity contest. After the Diana Saloon became Whiskey Row's main attraction in 1868, the Montezuma still kept up a steady business. It would also rival the Diana in terms of hosting bloodshed.

Surely the name "Montezuma" was coveted by any who would choose to run a drinking establishment on Montezuma Street. It's possible that it was the first solidly established saloon on this well-used dirt road when, with great excitement, George Holaday opened the Montezuma on lot 17, 108 Montezuma Street in mid-January 1866. His primary offerings, dealt by bartender Andrew "Jack" Shanks, were fine wines from California. Holaday's honeymoon with his saloon ended abruptly. On a Sunday night, February 11, 1866, extremely drunk soldiers from Fort Whipple got into a row in the Montezuma. Furniture was wrecked. Shots were fired. One bullet clipped a soldier's wrist. That was enough for Holaday, who abandoned the Montezuma and bolted to Calfornia the next day. It was assumed he was gone for good. Holaday, however, would return and prove himself a worthy Prescott pioneer.

Six months after this drunken soldier brawl, Holaday redeemed himself by opening the Pine Tree Saloon at 160 Montezuma Street, three doors north of Goodwin Street, lot 35, where Prescott's original post office had once been. The Pine Tree also had a twenty-four-hour bakery and coffee

In the 1880s, companies such as this one fought Whiskey Row fires, but before that, bucket brigades, formed on the spot, were relied upon. *Nancy Burgess.*

shop attached. However, at three in the morning of May 2, 1867, the ugly glimmer of flames was sighted inside Holaday's tavern. It and the theater next to it were destroyed, but the rest of the Prescott business district was saved by a determined bucket brigade. Holaday didn't rebuild.[65]

Cal Jackson was originally touted to run the saloon section of Albert Noyes's corner building that became the Diana. He would still become a key player in Prescott's row of saloons. He grabbed control of the Montezuma shortly after Holaday had fled Prescott. At that time, lot 17 was divided by a center wall into two saloons. The Exchange Saloon, John Baldwin as proprietor, was the other. Jackson and Baldwin joined forces in May; the partition was removed and the two saloons were consolidated into "a fine, large saloon," the Montezuma. In March 1868, Jack Shanks took over the "engineering" of the Montezuma with Nathaniel Pierce. They spruced it up nicely. Success was expected because "almost every vigorous Arizonian imbibes the kind of medicine sold by them." Still, Shanks and Pierce lasted only about four months. From then until January 1870, the Montezuma remained unstable. Constancy finally came when Charles Luke—future mayor of Prescott and uncle to the famous World War I flying ace Frank Luke—acquired it. Like several other saloon owners, Luke advertised the Montezuma as "the largest and most desirable resort in Prescott."[66]

Up until 1875, the Montezuma operated relatively trouble free. Then things changed. As if natural causes for fires weren't plentiful enough in Prescott, the occasional incendiary would rear his nasty soul. On Sunday night, December 26, 1875, "some miserant attempted to set fire in Prescott by kindling a blaze in the wood-pile in the rear of the Montezuma Saloon." The fire made some progress before it was discovered and was just about to attack the barn belonging to Luke. Fortunately, it was snuffed before this could happen.[67]

Occasionally, a fight that started inside a saloon was quashed by those nearby but continued away from the bar. Such was the case regarding a fatal affray that began in the Montezuma on the night of April 19, 1876. A U.S. Army musician, Albert Wienlewski, got into a quarrel with two other soldiers—one of them unnamed, the other a fellow musician, Carl Michel—"which through the interference of other parties was for the time quelled." Alone, Wienlewski headed back to his quarters at Fort Whipple. The two soldiers followed and, somewhere along the way, confronted him. The unnamed soldier removed his coat and challenged Wienlewski to a fistfight. Wienlewski responded by drawing a revolver and firing at the soldier. Michel, however, stepped between and took the bullet into his right side. Bleeding copiously, he clung to life for a half hour before closing his eyes forever.[68]

In 1883, Gilman Shaw, who'd formerly owned the Palace Saloon on Gurley Street that has been incorrectly linked with today's Palace Restaurant and Saloon, took over the Jackson & Tompkins' Saloon on 134 Montezuma Street. This establishment had been saved during the 1883 Whiskey Row fire by the barrier John Campbell's brick store had provided (see chapter 7). The Montezuma wasn't as fortunate. However, Shaw rechristened the old Jackson & Tompkins' the Montezuma Saloon. Shaw ran the Montezuma for four years and lured potential customers by inviting them to "Visit the halls of 'The Montezuma.'"[69]

Shortly after Shaw took over the Montezuma, a stabbing incident took place there on October 11. Two unidentified men, one from Lynx Creek and the other who lived in Prescott, had been arguing the night before. They decided to renew their fight the next afternoon in the Montezuma. When things got out of control between the two, Joe Taylor stepped in to attempt some peacemaking. By then, however, a knife had been drawn. Taylor turned away from it when he saw it coming toward his chest, but the knife struck him in the upper arm. This is one of several episodes on Whiskey Row whereby tragedy was averted by a sudden twist of body or circumstance.[70]

In less than one month, tragedy did find the Montezuma. During the morning of November 3, a man who'd been employed in Kirkland Valley, James Monroe—aka James Utley—visited several Whiskey Row bars while binge drinking. Several witnesses attested he'd been boasting that he intended to kill someone. Anyone. Just after one o'clock that afternoon, Monroe entered the Montezuma. He approached the bar and asked bartender L.W. Greenwell if he knew anyone in the mood to die. Greenwell offered the obvious response. Montezuma customer Jack Shae didn't like what he was hearing, so he started backing his way toward the door. This was all the provocation the excessively intoxicated Monroe needed. He pulled his pistol and fired a wild shot that lodged into the wall. Shae promptly turned and sprinted toward the door. Monroe fired a second shot. This bullet found its mark, hitting Shae in the back just below his ribs on the left side. He crumbled to the floor. Monroe was vigorously disarmed and apprehended.[71]

Shae was carried upstairs and, while being tended to by Dr. Frederick Ainsworth, acted baffled as to why Monroe had chosen him as his victim; he "disclaim[ed] knowing or ever seeing his would be murderer." When questioned shortly after the shooting, Monroe spoke "in a dazed kind of way." He thought Shae had shot twice at him, so he retaliated. Eyewitnesses refuted every bit of this.[72]

Dr. Ainsworth was unable to remove the bullet from Shae, which proved fatal. Although Shae wasn't considered "a good member of society," Monroe was convicted of cold-blooded murder and sentenced to be hanged. In late January 1884, the gallows were readied. People arrived from all over Yavapai County to see Monroe hanged. However, in the final hour, Judge William French called off the execution. A retrial didn't occur until June 26, 1885, when he was allowed to enter a plea of second-degree murder. Judge John Howard was skeptical but allowed it. Instead of the noose, Monroe was given twenty-five years in prison. Most Prescottonians strongly disagreed with this decision.[73]

William "Red" Dulin took over the Montezuma in January 1888. It became the Montezuma Saloon, Billiard Room and Lodging House. Dulin would later sell liquor and Schlitz beer wholesale from the Montezuma until sometime in 1891 when it closed and was replaced by a saddle and harness store.[74]

Jackson & Tompkins' Saloon

After giving up control of the Montezuma, Cal Jackson bought a building on 134 Montezuma Street in 1868 for $2,000, nine lots down from Moeller's corner spot. He quickly filled it with allurements he hoped would provide some competition for the Quartz Rock and Montezuma saloons and the soon-to-be-opened Diana Saloon. Jackson followed the trend of adding billiard tables to the mix, installing two. He also traveled to San Francisco and brought back the finest liquors available. He had two bartenders, Joe and Sol (Cal's brother), advertised as "the handsomest and noisiest men in town." Champagne was served from the tap with the promise that "We never slop over." Bartender Joe had a special drink called "Purp." Additionally, each ad enigmatically pointed out that Joe "now had another attraction." It was never revealed in print what that enticement was.[75]

In 1869, Jackson joined forces with his friend William "Doc" Tompkins. They simply called their place Jackson & Tompkins' Saloon. Jackson and Tompkins proudly advertised that they neighbored a store made of brick, which belonged to John Campbell. Fourteen years later, that fact proved fortunate. In 1883, the southward path of a roaring fire would be halted by Campbell's brick walls, saving several businesses on Whiskey Row, including Jackson & Tompkins'.[76]

In August 1873, a group of musical Kansan immigrants sojourned in Prescott for more than a week. On Saturday night, August 22, they took over the Plaza bandstand and began an impromptu recital, playing songs Prescottonians hadn't heard for some time. A large crowd assembled. For a brief but enchanting time, sentimentality overcame those present as they listened to the dulcet sounds coming from "bass viol, harp, violin and guitar." One ardent listener was Doc Tompkins. The Kansans asked for no donations, but when Tompkins asked them to continue their music-making in his bar, they admitted that it had been "a long time between drinks." A crowd followed the musicians into Jackson & Tompkins'. Several dozen bottles of champagne were emptied, "and the goose was properly elevated to a proper height." Pleasant news coming from a saloon wasn't rare on Whiskey Row. Like today, however, it was sensational events that made its way into print more regularly.[77]

In October 1877, what is perhaps Whiskey Row's most famous shooting incident occurred, primarily because it included future Wild West icon Virgil Earp. This episode would prove impactful on his career as a lawman, if not its launching point. It started at Jackson & Tompkins', but its genesis traced eight years back to Texas when Colonel William McCall—a Civil War hero who had risen to the rank of brevet brigadier general—learned of the murder of Robert Broddus, sheriff of Montague County. McCall moved to Prescott sometime after and stayed. George Wilson was the murderer, and now in Prescott as well. Broddus wasn't the only sheriff Wilson had killed. Unknown at the time, Wilson was also wanted in Colorado for the murders of the sheriff and deputy of Los Animas County. Furthermore, one of those Wild West curiosities was revealed when it was later learned that Wilson had an encounter with Virgil's younger brother, Wyatt, in 1875 in Wichita, Kansas. Wilson had failed to pay for a wagon he'd acquired. Wyatt, as a policeman, personally collected that debt. Although new to Arizona as a desperado, Wilson had been an outlaw on the loose for some time.

On Wednesday morning, October 17, McCall was playing a game of pool in Jackson & Tompkins' with every reason to believe he was far from harm's way. In walked three men—Wilson, Robert Tullos (aka John Tallos) and an unidentified third—clearly looking for McCall. Suddenly, he found himself sandwiched between two of them. One jabbed a pistol into McCall's back; the other applied "to him some obnoxious epithets." McCall recognized Wilson—who was calling himself "Mr. Vaughn"—the murderer of Broddus. McCall somehow escaped and reported Wilson's presence to justice of the peace C.F. Cate, who issued a warrant for the arrest of "Mr. Vaughn [Wilson] and John Doe [Tullos]." It was given to village marshal Frank Murray.

Just before Murray arrived at Jackson & Tompkins', one of the three men had shot at a dog. When Murray, accompanied by McCall, confronted Wilson and Tullos, the two thought they were being called to task for the attempted dog assassination. Wilson then suddenly pulled his pistol on Murray. Both Wilson and Tullos quickly betrayed their companion by blaming him for the animal abuse and ordered him to get on his horse and ride. Sensing things were about to get out of hand, Murray backed his way out of the bar. It took an hour before Murray was able to form a posse composed of U.S. marshal Wiley Standefer, Yavapai County sheriff Ed Bowers and Virgil Earp (identified in the *Miner* as "Mr. Earb"), who by fortunate circumstance were engaged in friendly conversation with one another somewhere on Whiskey Row. Earp was deputized on the spot. Colonel McCall agreed to take up the chase as well. Before this, Wilson and Tullos, fearing capture, had mounted their horses and, like a scene from so many Western movies, charged southward down Montezuma Street "at break neck speed shooting to the right and left as they went."[78]

The ensuing chase wasn't what this freshly formed, all-star posse expected. Standefer and McCall pursued in a horse-drawn carriage. Murray and Bowers followed on horseback, and behind them, on foot and toting a Winchester rifle, was Virgil Earp. With an hour's head start, a successful escape was probable. Rather, Wilson and Tullos dismounted and lingered near Albert Noyes's house, located on the southern edge of Prescott by Granite Creek. They reloaded their pistols and waited in plain view. The desperado Wilson apparently wanted to add another sheriff—or more—to his list of kills, and "no doubt felt officer proof, inasmuch as he had killed two sheriffs in his time and successfully eluded his pursuers in many a similar affair." Expecting the fugitives to still be running, Standefer and McCall rode right by them and might've missed them altogether had not one of them yelled, "Don't run over us, you s—of a b—."

After realizing who the men were, Standefer and McCall alit from their buggy, pistols drawn and cocked, and cautiously approached the outlaws. At the same time, Bowers and Murray rode up from the south. They, too, drew their guns. Somehow Earp had kept up on foot and set up at an angle between Standefer and McCall and Bowers and Murray. One of the latter two called out to Wilson and Tullos, demanding surrender. They were surrounded. Before the shooting started, Wilson was heard shouting an entreaty toward Heaven, "O' Lord have mercy on me, a poor drunken, worthless d—d s—of a b—." Wilson and Tullos opened fire. Bullets and buckshot came from three directions, with Earp "doing good service between the two fires." When the salvo ended, Wilson lay critically wounded from a bullet that had passed through his forehead and into his brain. Tullos lay dead from eight different wounds.

Wilson, to the astonishment of many, hung on for two days. The *Miner* boys turned theological after this, wondering if the prayer Wilson had bellowed before being shot would have any effect because of its sincerity, even with its profanity: "It was the language with which he was familiar. The question is, are not such earnest prayers as likely to be answered as those hypocritically expressed in more elegant phrase?"[79]

Almost three years later, during the Wednesday evening of November 17, 1880, Lester Jackson, who'd taken over his brother's saloon, got into an affray with teamster Barnabus Hussey. Fatality was avoided in Jackson & Tompkins' that night, but only fortuitously. What instigated the trouble isn't clear. At some point, Hussey attacked Jackson with a "deadly weapon." Such was the intensity of his assault that Jackson feared for his life, so he yanked his pistol—apparently of a high-powered variety—and fired two shots. The

Virgil Earp's career in law enforcement is believed to have begun on Whiskey Row. *Wikimedia Commons.*

first blast knocked out the lights leaving "the combatants in total darkness," which may've been Hussey's saving grace. Jackson's second shot passed through Hussey's hat, a mere inch from his temple. One observer reacted to the gunshots by diving toward the saloon door and wound up double-somersaulting onto Montezuma Street forty feet from the saloon. Hussey was thrown in jail but the next day was seen out and about, tending to business.[80]

As stated earlier, Jackson & Tompkins' Saloon survived the Whiskey Row Fire of 1883. Soon after, Gilman Shaw bought this establishment and renamed it the Montezuma Saloon.

THE CURSE OF THE KEYSTONE SALOON

The Keystone Saloon was situated in that area of early Whiskey Row that bled north onto Cortez Street. If any Whiskey Row saloon was cursed, it was the Keystone. Its ill-fated reputation began in 1884 when a lightning bolt struck and destroyed the barn attached to it. Everything in the barn was destroyed, including two horses stabled there. The real curse, however, began with its first proprietor. Gotlieb Urfer came to America from Canton of Bern, Switzerland, sometime before the American Civil War. He arrived in Prescott in 1874, opened a lodging house on Cortez in 1877 and married Ellen Dunn of Ireland in 1878. In 1882, Urfer bought the Arizona Brewery, one of Prescott's most popular gathering places. To his lodging house, however, he eventually added a saloon and named it the Keystone Saloon and Lodging House, which became his primary business.[81]

On Wednesday, December 16, 1885—one day before his fiftieth birthday—the Keystone proprietor was found lying senseless on the floor behind the bar, bleeding profusely from a bullet wound to the head. A Keystone lodger had sprinted into the saloon at about six o'clock after hearing the report of a pistol. However, he wasn't the first on the scene. A distraught and unidentified African American man was standing at the bar looking down at Urfer. The lodger also noticed a revolver lying on the floor, and Urfer had "a great ghastly hole in the right side of his head, from which his brains and blood were oozing." By the time the lodger turned to ask the man what had happened, he'd absconded. Several others who'd been nearby ran into the saloon. Therein they saw what the lodger was seeing, and "near his right hand, lay a pistol of the bull-dog pattern," a British-made pocket revolver—the same make used to assassinate President James Garfield in 1881. Those first on the scene, save for the Keystone lodger, immediately concluded this was a suicide.

Urfer's death was a scratch-your-head-and-wonder incident. Why would he kill himself? There were no signs he was on a path leading to such a horrifying terminus. Especially mystifying was that Urfer had been excitedly preparing for a grand celebration to be held in the Keystone. A few days before his death, an announcement appeared revealing not only his plans but also his apparent state of mind: "Gotlieb Urfer, the genial host of a lodging house and saloon, will celebrate his fiftieth birthday on Thursday, December 17th, and feels so jolly over the event that he wants all his friends to call and partake of a lunch which he will spread, from 1 o'clock to 4." Friends said that he'd even been talking about how he'd seat his guests.

On December 16, moments before the fatal shot was heard from the Keystone, he'd been preparing for the next day's feast. Mrs. Urfer had stepped out a short time ago. With him was George Hook, who Urfer asked to run out to buy some eggs. Less than five minutes later, Urfer was lying on the floor of his saloon in a pool of his own blood. In spite of these contexts, the physical evidence provided no other conclusion but that Urfer's death was self-inflicted. All other considerations were notional. The African American standing over Urfer had surely bolted because of the way it looked and was never seen again.

Not long after Urfer's suicide, an unidentified lodger made the same choice but used a different method: suicide by swallowing poison.[82]

The Keystone curse had only just begun. The drama would intensify. Thomas McCarron handled Urfer's estate and took over the Keystone's proprietorship. That's not all he took. Less than a year later, on Monday, November 14, 1886, McCarron married Urfer's widow. The *Miner* made sure to mention that McCarron's friends were stunned and that he'd married "Mrs. Urfer." Incidentally, the bride and groom were both considered wealthy.

Eight months later, another ineffable episode occurred with way too much déjà vu. Around two o'clock in the afternoon of Saturday, July 9, 1887, the crack of a gun was once again heard from the Keystone. Seconds later, another shot rang out. Passersby on Cortez ran in to see what had happened. There lay Ellen Dunn's second husband "with a ghastly hole in his right temple, from which his brains and life's blood lay fast oozing," less than ten feet from where his predecessor had shot himself through the head a year and a half before.

McCarron's choice of weapon was an antiquated cap-and-ball revolver with a barrel nearly a foot long. Oscar Vanderbilt was the first on the scene. Upon seeing McCarron's state, he rushed to get medical help, finding it in Dr. Robinson. When the doctor arrived, McCarron was still breathing but heavily. Death rattled in his throat. Forty-five minutes after he'd sent a bullet into his brain, McCarron took his last breath.

The note McCarron left behind was shocking and telling; it undoubtedly explained why Urfer had killed himself. It read, "I, John McCarron, am going to commit suicide; kill my wife and then kill myself. All caused by woman's abuse." By all indications, McCarron intended to fulfill both promises. A friend named McIntyre had been visiting McCarron frequently, and he indicated the Keystone owner had been drinking heavily as of late. During one conversation, McCarron, in his drunkenness, paradoxically spoke of his wife affectionately but followed it by pulling his pistol from his pocket and saying, "It will be my doom." On Saturday July 9, McIntyre overheard McCarron asking the former Mrs. Urfer if she'd like to accompany him on a buggy ride. She declined, excusing herself by claiming she was too busy. That decision saved her life. It was now or never for McCarron. Shortly after McIntyre left, McCarron walked into his saloon with his revolver. The path of the first shot revealed that he'd missed his mark widely, as if checking to see if his pistol was working properly; it passed high up on one of the saloon's walls and then through the ceiling before landing outside. The second shot penetrated McCarron's skull.

After McCarron was pronounced dead, an immediate inquest was ordered. Like Urfer, his death was ruled a suicide. The oddities continued when McCarron's body was buried next to Urfer's in Prescott's Citizen Cemetery. The *Miner*, with no attempt to camouflage sarcasm, stated that the twice widowed Ellen Dunn now had "two little mounds to keep green and to strew flowers over." The now infamous lady married once more and became Mrs. Cronin. Her third husband, a laborer named James, somehow outlived the supreme nag by twenty years.[83]

The Keystone Saloon survived. One would think it had accommodated enough death. Yet, although three suicides had taken place there, it hadn't hosted a homicide. That would change eight years later, all because of a dispute over seventy-five cents. Once again, some called it the most atrocious act ever perpetrated in Prescott up until that time. It surely ranks high in that regard.

Charles Hobart had previously lived and worked in Prescott as a porter at the Scopel Hotel on the corner of Montezuma and Goodwin Streets. He'd been arrested for robbery in February 1895 but was given leniency; all

Gotlieb Urfer and John McCarron were buried side by side so that their widow could have "two little mounds to keep green and to strew flowers over." *Norman Fisk.*

Hobart was required to do was leave town. This he did, but he returned to Prescott on Wednesday, October 23 of that year. He found a vacant room in the lodging quarters of the Keystone and paid in advance to John Miller, its new proprietor, a total of one dollar, reserving four nights at twenty-five cents each. During the night, the behavior of the unaccompanied Hobart turned repellant: he "soiled the room." Of course, this didn't please Miller—described as "one of the most quiet, peaceable and inoffensive men living"—especially after Hobart reneged the next morning on his four-night reservation and demanded a reimbursement for his unused nights, which amounted to seventy-five cents. The disgusted Miller refused. That amount would be the fee, he said, for having "to clean the room in the condition it was in when [Hobart] left it." Hobart then pulled out his abbreviated Winchester rifle, pointed it at Miller and demanded reimbursement. Somehow Miller was able to get away. He went straight to Chief of Police Steve Prince and reported the incident.

Prince found Hobart and immediately took him into custody. That same afternoon, he stood trial. Hobart was only convicted for drunk and disorderly conduct and fined five dollars. He wasn't so short of money as to be in need of an extra seventy-five cents, because he paid his fine and was released. Peculiarly, his gun was returned to him. The five-dollar fine didn't deter Hobart. He immediately took to the streets. Toting his Winchester, he attracted ample onlooker attention. Later in the day, Hobart visited the Kelly & Stephens retail store on the corner of Gurley and Montezuma Streets. There he bought some woolen clothes. He returned there on horseback just after dusk and asked to borrow an overcoat because, he mentioned, he had a long, cold ride ahead of him. This was refused. Hobart rode off but didn't leave town and apparently slept under the stars that night.

Hobart started the next afternoon by visiting the Palace Saloon, where he started drinking. At some point, he glanced at a clock and premeditatedly announced it was time for the "shooting match" to take place. When asked what he meant, he bluntly stated he was going to kill John Miller before eight o'clock. Those at the Palace didn't take him seriously and did nothing. Hobart, however, wasn't done drinking. He rode his horse up Montezuma, turned right on Gurley and headed to the Sazerac Saloon. There he continued the same threats. The Sazerac's Chinese chef, John Ross, overheard them and, knowing of the prior day's trouble between him and Miller, believed they weren't products of hot air. Ross hastened a messenger to Prince.

Hobart, however, beat the chief of police there. In fact, it may have taken an unfortunate amount of time to get the message to Prince. One witness later testified that he'd seen Hobart near the Keystone looking for his dog half an hour before he, whiskey crazed and angry, walked into the Keystone with his Winchester. Miller was facing the door, standing in the middle of the room between the bar and stove. Hobart shouted, "Now Miller, you son of a b—, I want your money or I'll kill you," but gave him no chance to respond. Hobart propped the gun on his shoulder and fired. The bullet struck Miller directly in the lower throat. The saloon owner collapsed to the floor and, with blood gushing from his wound, took a few desperate gasps and expired.

Two men sitting at the Keystone bar witnessed the murder: Armstrong Roseberry and William Sachs. The startled Sachs stood up when the rifle was fired. Hobart felt threatened by Sachs's movement, so he pointed the barrel at him and warned, "If you move, you son of a b—, I'll kill you, too." A click was heard as Hobart readied his rifle with another cartridge. The gunman backed his way out onto the sidewalk, turned and, in spite of his pronounced intoxication, skillfully mounted his horse and galloped northward on Cortez. He swung left onto Willis Street before heading up Granite Street and out of town.

Within ten minutes of Miller's death, Sheriff George Ruffner and his deputies began pursuit. Ruffner is arguably not only Arizona's most storied sheriff but also its most successful. This wasn't his most famous pursuit of an outlaw but most likely his first. The lanky, six foot four inch Ruffner and his posse combed the countryside with no success and rested at midnight. Telegraph messages were sent to other Yavapai County lawmen to be on the look for a six foot, one inch, 180-pound man riding a small bay horse. Hobart had a "sandy complexion and sand moustache." That night proved fruitless. At daylight, the posse hit the trail again. Along the way, Ruffner and his posse picked up some Indian trackers, which would prove a wise decision. It was soon determined that Hobart was now on foot and heading south toward Phoenix. By Saturday, he'd turned back toward the Bradshaw Mountains, thinking he was still on the road to Phoenix. On Sunday, his trail led to the Cy Curtis Ranch, which had a deserted house on it. Hobart holed up there. When Ruffner and his posse learned this, Ruffner asked a man he'd encountered along the way—a worker at the nearby Gladiator Mine—if he would try to goad Hobart from the house and into the open. The miner acceded. His task would prove easier than anticipated. With the posse in hiding, the man approached the house but stopped at the well in front of it to take in some water. That's all it took to get the disoriented Hobart outside.

With the Winchester he'd used to kill Miller in hand, Hobart questioned the miner about where the nearby roads led. The conversation ended, and the man sauntered away. Ruffner emerged from hiding and ordered Hobart to throw up his hands and surrender. Instead, the murderer raised his rifle to shoot the sheriff. Seeing this, Under Sheriff Joseph Dillon shouted from the other direction. Hobart wheeled, but Dillon and the other members of the posse beat him to the trigger. Shots came from every direction. Only one took effect: Dillon's buckshot knocked the rifle from Hobart's grasp and injured his right arm. The Keystone Saloon murderer surrendered.

By eleven o'clock that Sunday night, Ruffner's posse and Hobart were back in Prescott. The accused "was given a hearty meal, which he ate with a relish." He was then locked up to stand trial, set for Wednesday, November 13. Initially, Hobart tried to appear insane, but no one bought his act. Two lawyers were appointed to defend him, but he refused. The trial was moved one day ahead. The testimonies of eyewitnesses Sachs and Roseberry were all it took to bring a guilty verdict. Hobart wept when given the sentence of life imprisonment.[84]

That same year, the Keystone Saloon narrowly escaped being destroyed by fire. It was still there on July 14, 1900, the day of the Great Fire, but not

John Miller was murdered in his Keystone Saloon by Charles Hobart on October 25, 1895. *Norman Fisk.*

the day after. It's possible the Keystone was where the Great Fire was finally snuffed, the end of line.[85]

As mentioned, the original owner of the Keystone, Gotlieb Urfer, also owned the popular Arizona Brewery, most likely the first beer brewery in Prescott, for a short time. Early breweries played a unique role in Whiskey Row history.

Chapter 6

Early Beer Breweries of Whiskey Row

A Short History

It's worth repeating that for a town famous in part because of a row named after whiskey, there was much initial opposition in Prescott to that preferred and potent beverage and the drinkers of it. It's pointless to argue there was no good reason for it. Truly, whenever there was a law-keeping problem in frontier Prescott, whiskey was often behind it. An 1869 *Miner* report expressed the desire that "those who will drink it do so like gentlemen, in small doses." Since this wish wouldn't always be granted, alternatives were sought. Besides all-out temperance, another choice was favored by many: beer, that tasty beverage of much less potency.[86]

Prescott's first two breweries were launched in 1867 about the time the territorial capital was moved to Tucson. The first to advertise was the Arizona Brewery and Saloon, situated on Gurley Street directly north of the Plaza in part of the old capital building. Its primary proprietor was John Littig. Littig lasted in Prescott only until 1870. He, with Prescott's justice of the peace, Samuel Blair, fled to Colorado after both swindled almost every person in town. The Arizona's competition, the Pacific Brewery on South Montezuma Street, was originated nearly the same time by John Raible and Phillip Sheerer. Raible was the driving force behind the Pacific and would be for nearly twenty-four years.[87]

Getting positive publicity came easier for beer brewers than whiskey sellers. The boys at the *Miner* had a weakness for lagers and ales, and the brewers knew it. Hence, Littig and Raible often brought samples of their latest batches to the *Miner* office for a tasting. It cannot be said it was

The Arizona Brewery moved into the old capital building on Gurley Street, shown here, in 1867. *Library of Congress.*

absolutely free advertising since a product was exchanged for a service; out of appreciation, a blurb would appear in the local section of the *Miner* touting the goodness of their homebrewed elixirs. A negative review was never given. Free beer for a few good words in print paid off for both sides. Littig began the practice in 1867, but it was particularly effective for John Raible and his Pacific Brewery after the *Miner* moved headquarters from Gurley to South Montezuma Street in the 1870s. Raible's malt mill then adjoined the *Miner* office.

After Littig ran for the hills, Jesse Jackson took over the Arizona Brewery. Still, the newspaper egged on competition. In July 1871, the *Miner* sneaked in a challenge by humorously asserting, "Jesse Jackson, of the Arizona, thinks his beer better than that of Raible & Sheerer's, of the Pacific, but we'll wager a small sum that he cannot take as much of his own medicine, as John Raible can of his, cause you see, his 'boiler' isn't as capable as John's." This friendly rivalry was short-lived. Jackson sold the Arizona to Julius Rodenburg and Gray Foster in 1872. Rodenburg, "a master brewer," was its backbone. He took over sole proprietorship in 1877, kept it until 1882 and, according to the *Courier*, made it into a "daisy." In 1881, Rodenburg became more interested in bringing the railroad to Prescott rather than good beer, so he sold the brewery to Gotlieb Urfer.[88]

The Arizona Brewery might've been the happiest place in Prescott in 1882, which adds more irony to Urfer's manner of death. Although Urfer

In this rare image, the popular Arizona Brewery can be seen just to the left of the Prescott Market. *Nancy Burgess.*

was Swiss, his brewery was regularly visited by a close-knit contingent of Germans. The editor of the *Miner*, Charles Beach, wrote, "Last Saturday evening while engaged in answering letters, sounds of vocal and instrumental music reached our well developed ears. A happy party of Germans across the way, in Urfer's, were letting themselves loose. Their performances were so good that we really forgot, for the time being, that people, although not rich, can be happy in this world, and there are, seemingly, no happier people than the Germans." The Arizona eventually became the Headquarters Saloon, co-owned by Fritz Jesson. The other owner was Valentine Riehl, a violent man who at one time was thought to have been killed in May 1889 by his lover, known as English Rose, after he attacked her. Instead, Riehl resurfaced in June and was sent to San Quentin for two years for nearly beating English Rose to death.[89]

By the middle 1870s, beer breweries in Prescott were a source of immense local pride. A report in 1878 declared that 25,327 gallons of beer had been manufactured in Arizona Territory during that year. Prescott was responsible for more than 9,000; Tucson—Prescott's competition at the time for Arizona Territory's most important city— produced only 2,000 gallons. Early Prescott was a whiskey town, but it was quite the beer town as well. There were at least three breweries in Prescott, all operated by first-class men, which meant first-class beer was being produced. In the late spring of 1879, the *Miner* reported, "Prescott

John Raible's Pacific Brewery had the advantage of adjoining the *Miner* headquarters where beer lovers worked. *Sharlot Hall Museum.*

brewers are busy all the time and barely supply the increasing demand for good lager. Three breweries in constant operation will give the readers an idea of the amount of beer used in this section."[90]

The *Miner* boys continued to use the power of their media to compare locally brewed beers in a way that, when viewed chronologically, manifests a humorous pattern. They knew samples would keep coming if they played their cards right. One week, the Excelsior's Brewery, whose proprietor was a master brewer named Luis Dugas, was concocting the best brew. The next, it was the Arizona or Raible's. More than once all three were touted as the best in one *Miner* edition. Over time, however, it was Raible's Pacific Brewery that proved the frontrunner the other two chased. It was Raible's ambition

---

PACIFIC ! BREWERY.

MONTEZUMA STREET,

South of the store of Ja's Grant.

RAIBEL & SHEARER, Proprietors.

Good LAGER BEER, Liquors and Cigars, always on hand.

As we brew our own beer, and take great pains in having it O. K., lovers of that healthy and strengthening beverage will do well to give us a call.   v4n24   RAIBEL & SHEARER.

The Pacific Brewery promoted its beer as being good for the body. *Sharlot Hall Museum.*

and pride as a native German beer-maker that drove him day and night to the top of Prescott's brewery heap.[91]

John Raible was born in Germany in 1833. After arriving in Prescott in 1864, he was given the contract, along with Dan Hatz and future swindler Samuel Blair, to construct the Governor's Mansion, which today forms the heart of the Sharlot Hall Museum campus. Carpentry, however, wasn't his larger calling. He shared proprietorship of the Pacific Brewery over the years, but he was not only the constant there but also the brainpower behind the business, always aiming to improve its beer-making capacity both in quality and quantity. Raible even promoted his product as "wholesome" and a "healthy, strengthening beverage."[92]

As the Pacific Brewery progressed, those at the *Miner* found Raible's efforts captivating. One report laughed, "The brewer has a new way of shutting off steam at John Raible's malt mill, when he wants to stop the machine he sings wo-o-o and the machine stops. It is not always quite so easy to start it again as he sometimes has to punch up the power with a sharp stick." Raible implemented a malt-crushing machine, a bottle washing machine that could clean three hundred bottles in one minute and a kiln for drying malt in a 324-square-foot room—he could dry up to 2,500 pounds of barley in there. Always trying to stay ahead of the game, he bought a massive, $200 icebox to store beer during summers. By 1880, he had his own "illuminated labels" on his beer bottles.[93]

The *Miner* men were in love with the idea of superior beer brewing in Prescott and viewed it as a lovely process: "We were conducted into John Raible's brewing cellar and allowed to behold a large tank of beer in its highest state of fermentation." There on the surface of the beer was white foam. The whole sight reminded them of "a mountain covered with silvery snow." By 1881, Raible was a wealthy man. His success fell right into the cauldron of Prescott's big city dreams. Of all the growing cities in Arizona, Prescott, with its cooler climate, was believed to have the most conducive environment for brewing beer. Raible's Pacific Brewery had grown in size and production, and its products were of a quality high enough that it was thought that "importation of beer from the States a thing of the past." Raible was already selling beer in Flagstaff, Verde Valley and the Palace Station, a stagecoach station midway between Prescott and the mines in the Bradshaw Mountains. One delivery of Pacific Brewery beer to the Palace Station caused the boys there to mistake "the day for the 4th of July, St. Patrick's or some other great and eventful day."[94]

Although Prescott undoubtedly had the best breweries in Arizona, much of the beer its citizens imbibed was exported from beer meccas such as Milwaukee, Chicago and St. Louis. Raible had been experimenting for some time with Arizona barley, especially that grown in the Salt River Valley. He considered it superior to that grown in the states or California and believed it produced a better malt. In the late winter of 1881, Raible traveled to St. Louis for the purpose of bringing another master brewer to Prescott. This "follower of Gambrinus" was soon "manufacturing beer pronounced equal to anything produced in the states." Why? This new brewer agreed with Raible, averring that the barley from Arizona "contain[ed] much saccharine matter and surpasses States' malt." Grandiose thoughts followed these revelations. With the railroad coming and the beer divine, why not think about making enough to export Prescott beer far and wide? Prescott could join the ranks of the major beer brewing cities and be known for its quality beer across the land.[95]

Just when Raible was ready to make his big push, efforts to bring the railroad to Prescott stalled. Then tragedy befell the Raibles when their infant son died in 1882. That same year, Raible was also distracted by politics. In August, he announced he was putting himself on the Republican ticket for the House of Representatives. By then, the *Courier* was up and running. Its editor John Marion, a stalwart Democrat, immediately started badmouthing Raible, calling him a "bloated capitalist." In the past, Marion, as editor of the *Miner*, had been the biggest fan of Raible's beer. Perhaps they had a heart-to-heart, or maybe he became concerned he wouldn't be getting any more free samples soon from the Pacific Brewery, because within three days, Marion recanted, calling Raible the only solid candidate on the Republican ticket. Raible's bid for that office fell short, but he would serve as city councilman, delegate to the Republican convention and in "other various positions of trust" over the years. Such was the respect for Raible that he was urged to run for mayor in 1887. It was his beer, however, that Prescottonians loved best, still said to be "purer and better than any that is imported."[96]

For a man of his prominence, Raible's ability to stay controversy-free was notable. In 1883, even when it did find him, it was of a mellower nature. Reporting it, Marion of the *Courier* started with, "A brewery is not, generally speaking, the sweetest smelling place in the world. John has tried to keep his place fresh and attractive. This we know, for we published the *Miner* for seven years next door to him." Near Raible's brewery, the city had been digging a ditch in preparation for placing a better sewer system along Montezuma Street. In the process, his "slopway" to Granite Creek was destroyed. Yes, Raible was allowed to dump the Pacific's waste into Granite Creek, but now it was being diverted to Montezuma Street, which was illegal. After Raible's trough to the creek was demolished, the city demanded that Raible fix it. He refused, because after all, he didn't wreck it. So the city took Raible to court. Marion suggested a solution; the brewery waste should be collected and used for fertilizer in the splendid vegetable gardens of Prescott's Chinatown on West Granite Street. Marion also suggested that the city "buy a barrel of John's best beer, treat all hands and refix that sewer." Lawyer Edmund Wells represented Raible. On August 31, a jury ruled in favor of Raible. The city was forced to repair his spillway to Granite Creek. Whether or not the workers consumed any of Raible's beer while doing so wasn't disclosed.[97]

The Pacific Brewery wasn't immune to Whiskey Row's greatest enemy: fire. In March 1884, a spark from a neighboring business nearly set it ablaze. It was caught in time. Three months later begot a different outcome. Around 8:30 during the evening of June 16, fire broke out in the engine room toward the rear of the *Miner* office. That portion of the building was quickly swallowed by flames. As Whiskey Row fires are prone to do, it traveled north. It was immediately discerned that the Pacific, adjoined to the northern wall of the *Miner* office, was doomed, but perhaps blowing it up would stop the blaze's advance. So it was. To onlookers, this produced quite a spectacle: "The explosion carried the fragments of the building high into the air, and the patter of the falling timbers as they came down was like the rattle of musketry." The dynamiting checked the fire. For a moment, it was thought the front end of the *Miner* building could be saved. That hope was extinguished after flames erupted through several areas of the roof. Firemen applied a steady stream from the well on the corner of Goodwin and Montezuma Streets and eventually tamed the fire, but not before the entire *Miner* office had been devoured. Much of Raible's beer-making equipment had been either pulled out in time or salvaged. By the end of July, he'd rebuilt and was brewing Whiskey Row's best beer again.[98]

Raible retired in 1886 but came back a year later to brew beer until 1891. In that year, the Pacific Brewery became the Pacific Saloon under Pat Barret. Barret later moved up the street to Block 13, reopening the Gem Saloon, one of Whiskey Row's earliest dating back to 1867. Raible passed away on June 1, 1899, from edema caused by cirrhosis of the liver. He was sixty-six years old. The legendary brewer was eulogized as an exemplary citizen and a true friend to many. Raible was especially remembered for always paying respect to Prescottonians who'd lost a loved one: "Few funerals ever occurred at which he was not present." His kindnesses were reciprocated when, in death, he was honored as one of Prescott's most influential pioneers. Today, his influence cannot be overrated. Raible's beer proved Prescott could do what big cities do.

BEER BREWERY STORIES PROVE DIFFERENT THAN WHISKEY SALOON STORIES: FOUR EXAMPLES

Proof of how tightly knit the Prescott community was in its early days and that friends often gathered in its breweries occurred in mid-December 1875. It was the night after Dan Hatz, the owner of one of Prescott's first boardinghouses, as well as the Oriental Bakery and Saloon on the corner of Montezuma and Goodwin Streets, was married. Hatz had a feeling his friends from the Pacific Brewery might drop by to do some serenading. In preparation, Hatz had bought some of Raible's beer for private use, hoping it'd make it easier to smile when the racket came; his friends apparently weren't capable of aesthetically pleasing intonations. Hatz, however, was touched when he saw his friends, already well-hydrated with Raible's beer themselves, marching toward his house because there in the front was his dog joyfully leading the way and howling as out of tune as any man there. Hatz later retorted that since his "dog didn't drink beer," he thought there was no reason he couldn't have a little fun "making the night hideous at his master's expense."[99]

For the most part, stories of a jollier ilk emanated from Prescott's brewery-saloons than its many whiskey dramshops. The Pacific Brewery was the site for most of them. It had many loyal regulars who met to do nothing but enjoy what was probably Prescott's best locally brewed beer and to share stories. Two men of German descent were doing just that on Saturday afternoon, August 27, 1876. One, a baker, was called Buffalo Joe. The other was identified only as Frankel. Both were known for being "a terror in that line" when it came to blue-streak talking. On this day, they used their mother tongue, exclusively, to converse. Several humans privy to their dialogue were said to have "escaped with their lives" by moving out of earshot of the Germans. A black dog, also of German pedigree, wandered by and stopped to listen to Buffalo Joe and Frankel: "The dog was brought up in a German school and understood the language." For about an hour, the canine sat below the two men as if intently listening. Suddenly the dog began to tremble and soon dropped dead at the foot of Raible's signpost. The cause? He was talked to death. "Strangers may doubt this story, but those acquainted with the loquacious powers and persistence of the parties will hardly be astonished at the result."[100]

Still, even Whiskey Row's happy-go-lucky beer taverns and breweries had Wild West–type troubles. Beer, however, wasn't usually a major part of their root causes like whiskey was for saloons. During the afternoon of November 24, 1876, a soldier from Fort Whipple who'd been inhaling benzene, a dangerous petroleum hydrocarbon that today is an ingredient in methamphetamine, lost his senses and went on a rampage down Montezuma Street. His motive was unrevealed, but he made a beeline for the Pacific Brewery with the intent to attack Raible's bartender and butcher. This multi-tasker, however, saw the soldier coming and grabbed his preferred weapon, a baseball bat. A fight followed. The bat-swinging barkeep won the battle, but it took several blows to the head to scare the soldier away. But the benzene-bloated trooper wasn't down for the count yet. Getting his second wind, he headed south, where he'd heard there were two other soldiers with whom he had a previous beef. The bat beating apparently didn't lessen the angry soldier's strength, because after finding the objects of his rage, he "polished them off nicely." Somehow, Marshal James Dodson was able to pacify and arrest him. Dodson then crammed him into the Prescott paddy wagon and deposited the benzene fiend in the county jail. On the way there, the driver noted that the soldier was the bloodiest human being he'd ever seen and that, clearly, "peace disturb[ed] his mind."[101]

One of the ugliest and most bizarre accidents in Prescott history also occurred in the Pacific Brewery. John Messerle was a brewer for Raible who'd recently come from Tucson. While working one day in October 1883, Messerle began sampling his own brew. At some point he fell into the "boiling vat" of potential lager. Several minutes passed before his absence was noticed, and "he was pulled out, more dead than alive." Dr. Robinson was promptly called on, who immediately unclothed the man and applied hopeful remedies. Already, Messerle's skin was peeling away from his body. Robinson applied raw cotton to the scalded wounds and covered him with blankets. Messerle wasn't expected to live. No updates, however, appeared in either of Prescott's newspapers.[102]

When John Raible retired, the Prescott beer brewing craze dwindled. Along the way, saloons were still the rulers of Whiskey Row. There were so many—some that came and went, some that dug themselves in and stayed for years—that documenting all of them is an impossibility. The next section, however, describes a few more.

Honorable Mention Saloons

In 1875, Hughey's Saloon stood on one of the corners of Gurley and Granite Streets. It claimed to sell the best beer on the planet, mostly imports from St. Louis. The grandiosity continued. Hughey's avowed that "Regular Patrons Live Long and Never Grow Gray Hairs." This make-believe fountain of youth then added an imperative, "Don't forget the place," as if the promise of unparalleled beer and long life weren't enough.[103]

Appearing in the early 1880s was the Parlor Saloon, stationed on lot 27, 140 Montezuma Street, and operated by William "Billy" Vernon from Washington, D.C. Vernon's goal was to make the Parlor a place for sophisticates to gather. Along with the finest liquors available, it had the best cigars in town. Havanan cigars specifically labeled for the Parlor were "made of the finest leaf possible." Inside the saloon were stylish paintings and Brussels carpeting. Vernon himself was first-class, one who'd work himself to exhaustion and even sickness. In fact, when he died of pleurisy in the late winter of 1882 at the age of forty, some attributed the cause to his unmatched work ethic.[104]

Captain Paul "P.M." Fisher, was given control of Billy Vernon's estate, including the Parlor. Fisher rented it to Charles Keyes. Vernon's aim to make the Parlor a sophisticated resort was honored and maintained. It was "quiet and orderly, where any person can enter without being terrified with hideous squalling or rather roaring." Keyes's stint at the Parlor was short-lived. L.P. Davis bought Keyes out and operated the saloon until shortly after catastrophe struck Whiskey Row in 1883. The Parlor, however, wasn't a victim. A few months after the fire, proprietorship of the Parlor changed again, as did its name. Alexis Boyle, called "Sport" by his friends, took control of the Parlor in October 1883 and renamed it Cob Web Hall.[105]

Boyle's tenure at the Cob Web was short. Later, he bartended at the Fashion Saloon on Gurley Street. In the early morning of Saturday, June 6, 1891, Boyle stepped behind the bar of the Fashion and noticed the safe's door was ajar. Seeing what was in it proved too tempting, especially since no one else was in the bar. Ignoring the consequences, Boyle grabbed a sack containing $800 worth of silver and ran out to the street. There he wrapped it in a pair of overalls and stashed it away. Somewhere along the way, Boyle realized the foolishness of his impulsive act and wanted to undo it, but it was too late. Around four o'clock that morning, Frank Mayfield, the night bartender of the Fashion noticed the door of the safe was still unlocked. Gone was the silver. He recalled that the only other person who'd been behind the bar that day was Sport Boyle. The senior partner of the Fashion, P.L. Kastner, gave this information to Sheriff James Lowery. He promptly arrested Boyle and lodged him in jail. Kastner threatened prosecution should Boyle fail to reveal the silver's hiding place. This weakened the former Cob Web Hall proprietor, who then led Kastner and a deputy sheriff to the cache. Leniency was shown the generally law-abiding Sport Boyle. All was forgiven and further jail time avoided.[106]

In Boyle's place stepped an even more charismatic character, P.M. Fisher. In terms of personality, Fisher was at the head of the class. Another who'd come west after heeding the call of California gold, he headed to southern Arizona in the early 1860s. There he became a steamboat merchant on the lower Colorado River, where he earned his sobriquet, "Captain." He moved to Prescott in 1877. One friend claimed he was "an exceptionally interesting and engaging character" who attracted to the Cob Web "the best of the saloon-going element." Fisher offered billiards, fine liquors and, like Billy Vernon, cigars especially made for the Cob Web, noted for their unusually sweet flavor. Edmund Wells—who would become a key figure in creating Whiskey Row lore—called it "the most strictly high-grade saloon" on Whiskey Row, "the loitering center of artists and men of world travel, and learned men, intermingling the characteristics of different countries, sects, and peoples."[107]

The Plaza Bit Saloon—which would use more than one name—stood on lot 35, 160 Montezuma Street. There, the future Whiskey Row icon, the twenty-something Barney Smith, began his career as a saloonkeeper. Smith,

Barney Smith brought bowling to Whiskey Row in his Plaza Bit Saloon. *Sharlot Hall Museum.*

one of the savviest businessmen Whiskey Row would ever know, brought bowling to Prescott at the Plaza Bit. Yet his saloon, it was said, could have passed for an art gallery. Smith ambitiously worked to make the Plaza Bit a match for the Cabinet Saloon, which he would someday co-own. Smith also provided a gambling room where gentlemen could "slip in at the back door, play off or win a few hundred and no one [would] know what has happened." His Plaza Bit brought such a profit that in 1879, Smith was able to purchase a year's supply of liquor in advance, which was extremely valuable in a remote, pioneer town.[108]

The Sazerac on Gurley Street was owned by George Sines. Sines was unique among saloon owners because he was a skilled hunter, which meant he provided inexpensive fresh meat, especially venison, for the restaurant portion of the Sazerac. For some reason, the Sazerac was a frequent target of Salvation Army anti-saloon missionaries, perhaps because of its ideal location on Gurley Street.

The Central Saloon was a short-lived but busy saloon on Montezuma Street. George Yackle offered Cuban cigars, good liquors, music, games and other amusements in "quarters [that were] large, airy and cool." In his advertisement, if one reads the bold print only, Yackle presented a not so subliminal message: "A MAN AT THE CENTRAL SALOON WANTS TO SPEAK TO YOU PROVIDED YOU BRING CASH!"[109]

A MAN

can buy as good Liquors for a Bit a Drink

AT THE

CENTRAL SALOON

as are sold elsewhere for a quarter of a dollar, or as fine a Havana Cigar as anybody

WANTS

to smoke at the same price, so

TO SPEAK

I take this method of saying

To You

that my new quarters are large, airy and cool. All sorts of games for pleasure are

PROVIDED

for the amusement and pleasure of

YOU

and for all of your friends you

BRING.

I am selling First-Class Goods, and no other, and therefore must have

CASH !

☞ Music every Evening.

GEO. S. YACKLE,

PROPRIETOR.

MONTEZUMA STREET - - PRESCOTT.

George Yackle had a creative way of advertising his Central Saloon. *Sharlot Hall Museum.*

Chapter 7

Whiskey Row's Embellishment Wars and the James Dodson Era

After opening in 1874, it didn't take long for Dan Thorne's Cabinet Saloon to become the powerhouse of Whiskey Row. "Let the times change as they may, [it] always has a full house. The 'Cabinet' does more business than any similar house east of San Francisco," stated an 1879 report. By then, Prescott was dreaming of becoming a big city. Progress, however, was marked not by how many buildings went up but how their quality compared with those found in established larger cities, especially San Francisco. There were always hopes that something palatial would be erected. The Cabinet had the best chance of getting there first. In March 1878, Thorne stopped everything and decided to have the Cabinet "completely overhauled, renovated, transmogrified, turned upside down, and inside out." When finished, it was said it would "likely be mistaken for the Laurel Palace or some other city institution." Thorne worked quickly. The Cabinet reopened with a bang on Saturday evening, March 30. According to the *Miner*, it was now equal to "the best saloons in San Francisco." A huge crowd, "as usual," gathered. It was composed mostly of miners and especially "bonanza kings." Money was spent liberally, "just as miners generally do."[110]

Thorne was never satisfied with the status quo and was constantly reinventing the Cabinet. Between 1874 and 1883, it was closed for repairs and improvements at least five times. Because Prescott was still a young and growing frontier town, improvements in quality were always newsworthy, even regarding what now seems simple. An addition outside of the Cabinet made news in 1882: "D.C. Thorne's Cabinet saloon, Montezuma Street is now lighted in front by a large, brilliant and handsomely painted lamp. It is an aesthetic affair." That same year, it was even reported that the Cabinet had a new storm door.[111]

Thorne constantly toyed with ways to keep his saloon Whiskey Row's center of activity; he needed more than a cabinet full of valuable rocks on display. This included a chophouse run by the much respected Chinaman George Ah Fat. Even though his primary clientele consisted of rugged miners, the Cabinet also offered "fancy drinks." There was Gold Lion Whiskey, Mountaineers, brandy smashes, wine on ice, Cabinet punches, milk punches, imported ginger ale and Apollinaris water—spring water from Bad Neuenahr, Germany. The Cabinet was also often host to a weekly lottery. In 1881, a grand lottery for a $25 prize was held at the Cabinet every Saturday at eight o'clock in the evening. A ticket came when one purchased his first drink of the night. The source of the prize money was explained in a weekly ad in the *Miner*: "Being desirous of dividing some of the money made out of [Thorne's] Silver Belt mine, the best in the country, the proprietor of the 'Cabinet' takes this method of unloading." There was the occasional raffle, like that for a "fine black horse, formerly owned by Major Trowler." Two hundred tickets were sold at $1.50 each.[112]

Thorne, with another saloon proprietor, had another idea that was implemented in 1880–81 that brought some short-term excitement on Whiskey Row.

COCKFIGHTING COMES TO WHISKEY ROW

By 1880, Prescott's reputation throughout Arizona was that it had become so law-and-order as to be almost dull. While a matter of pride for most, it nevertheless caused some slight embarrassment among those of a rowdier frontier spirit. Two of them were Thorne and J.A. "Scotty" Scott, who'd purchased the Plaza Bit Saloon and renamed it the Plaza Bar, Billiard Saloon and Ten Pin Alley (often simply called the Bowling Alley Saloon by locals). Their remedy? The world's oldest spectator sport. Cockfighting. Scott took the lead by announcing "that there really was to be a genuine cock-fighting in staid and moral old Prescott." The first event opened near Scott's bowling alley at eight o'clock during the Wednesday evening of December 22, 1880. A throng of "sporting men" attended. Eight specially bred fighting roosters were brought in for four separate duels. The fourth battle was the marquee matchup. It featured "a red Irish game cock and a [D]ominique, the [D]ominique with heels and the game without." Having heels seemed to matter little as the feisty Irish rooster pinned the Dominque against the wall for the win. The event was a massive hit, leaving participants and spectators begging for an encore. More than $500 changed hands.[113]

The reprise took place on a Friday evening, January 25, 1881. It topped the first contest in terms of attendance, money, excitement and blood. Two roosters were killed. And there was controversy. Thorne had entered his own Irish stag (a rooster under one year old) for the main fight. Betting was high, and a few men tried to rig the fight against Thorne's athlete, who would have

Rally!   Rally!
——TO THE——
GRAND OPENING
—OF—
The Cock Pit!
Friday Evening, Dec. 23,
Over the Cabinet Restaurant, to commence with a
General Maine of Game Cocks,
To be followed by Match Fights.
☞ DOORS OPEN AT 7 O'CLOCK. ☜
dec21-3t

Dan Thorne featured cockfights above the Cabinet Restaurant in 1881. *Sharlot Hall Museum.*

none of it. To the delight of most in the crowd, the Irish stag "knocked the life" out of its opponent.[114]

Cockfighting went on hiatus for the rest of 1881, perhaps because Thorne was out of town for several months on a trip back east. He was back in September and making "things 'talk' at the Cabinet." Toward the end of December 1881, Thorne announced the creation of "The Cock Pit," stationed on the roof of the Cabinet Restaurant behind the saloon. Inaugural night was scheduled for December 23 at seven o'clock. A fight between two gamecocks that had fought a year ago at Scotty Scott's January event, Daly and Murphy, made up the featured matchup for a purse of $100. The event, as expected, was well attended. The money waged and taken at the door was considerable, especially "for a town of this size." Even though gamecocks Daly and Murphy were pulled from the lineup, four fights took place that thrilled those present. The second battle, which lasted thirty minutes, was the highlight. It featured roosters Garfield and Grant. Grant upset the favorite by killing him. The cockfights may have continued, but the December 23 games were the last to be reported.[115]

THORNE INITIATES AN EMBELLISHMENT WAR

D.C. Thorne wasn't the only saloon man pushing to improve the quality of his resort. Ironically, after all the anti-saloon and whiskey talk, after the lawlessness for which they were blamed, it was Prescott's saloons that now compared most favorably with big-city edifices. Once the shame of Prescott, its saloons were now its pride. Because of their quality and the work put into making them that way, they were used as signs of progress and proof of catching up to larger cities.

The reopening of the Cabinet on March 30, 1878, was an early salvo in what might be called an "embellishment war." The late 1870s and 1880s yielded a new era for Prescott. Law and order became the norm. A spirit of upgrading caught fire along Whiskey Row among saloon proprietors. "Improvement is the motto of our business men," shouted the *Miner*. The Diana—now run by "the prince of saloon proprietors," Joe Crane—wasn't about to give up her "queen of Whiskey Row" status without an honest fight. Prescott's big-city longings surfaced again when reports of the Diana's improvements were published in June 1878. The ten-year old bar was now "in a shape that would be hard to beat in larger cities." The Diana's augmented ornamentation included "new fixtures [and] brilliant gas lights" and a cabinet full of top-line liquors and cigars.[116]

The Cabinet and Diana both added quality music to their respective offerings. The Diana often featured high-class violinists and harpists; Thorne countered by bringing in a $600 piano, a hefty price during this time. In 1881, the Cabinet became almost unrivaled when it added a restaurant and went on the European plan. The waiters in both the restaurant and saloon were called polite and "of genteel appearance." It was designed for those who were "fond of good living." For the Cabinet to be challenged as the king of Whiskey Row, it would require a completely new establishment built from scratch. As will be seen, that saloon appeared in 1883.[117]

In late April 1880, during Crane's stint as proprietor of the Diana—now considered "the popular old 'stand by'"—a self-proclaimed billiard master came to Prescott. Calling himself Willie Brown, he strutted into the Diana and issued a challenge to any Prescottonian thinking himself worthy to play him and willing to ante up the appropriate amount of money for a match. Frank Murphy, who would later play a significant role in bringing the railroad to Prescott, accepted. Brown and Murphy squared off in Crane's domain on a Friday evening. Much to Brown's embarrassment, he lost to Murphy in a game to three hundred points. He wouldn't go down easy; he challenged Murphy to a rematch, which transpired the following Sunday evening. This time Murphy whipped Brown even worse, beating him by fifty-five points. The "billiard sharp" slunk out of Prescott poorer and hoping the whole affair would remain unreported.[118]

Whiskey Row now exemplified Prescott's growth and prosperity. Of course, neither of these ideals were possible without law and order. William Jennings had proven it was advantageous to have a feared man prowling Whiskey Row to uphold the law. James Dodson was the next rung in that ladder. He was the right man in the right place at the right time. Dodson has already been referred to in this book. Now is a good time to interject a fuller history of the man who quieted Whiskey Row. There was plenty of noise, however, along the way.

THE DODSON ERA

"Prescott has five churches and two school buildings, 18 saloons, two breweries, a City Marshal, is the Capital of the Territory, county seat of Yavapai, and is soon to be lighted with gas," read the *Miner* on March 10, 1882. The "City Marshal" listed here as one of Prescott's sources of pride was James Dodson. After William Jennings was ousted from his night watchman post in 1877, the next lawman of note was Dodson, whose achievements have been largely overlooked by those who've chronicled the history of Arizona, let alone the American West. Arguably, Dodson should be listed alongside legends such as William Hickok or the Earp brothers, men who've occupied innumerable pages of written history. He was certainly as effective as these men—if not more so—comparably colorful, equally bold and less controversial. Perhaps it was this latter quality or that he never wrote an autobiography that has left him relatively unheralded. While living, however, it was known by early Prescottonians that he was "a born guardian of the peace, and there are few men in the west who have done more good service than he has."[119]

The people of early Prescott venerated Dodson and expressed their gratitude for him often. The *Miner* said of him: "Politically he differs with the *Miner*, but in sense of duty is in perfect accordance. Through his firmness Prescott is saved many riotous scenes. James is genial and kind in his everyday intercourse with his fellow man, but when it comes to duty he knows no one, and in this particular he is a perfect brick." Another report stressed that he made "bad characters understand there is a God in Israel." Because of Dodson—who "seldom permitted a row to ripen"—Prescott never became as lawless as some other frontier towns such as Deadwood, Dodge City or Tombstone. But make no mistake, Prescott hosted just as many if not more dubious characters. Young Prescott was a whiskey and gambling town. That

James Dodson, Whiskey Row's peacemaker, has been largely ignored by Western historians. *Sharlot Hall Museum.*

combination eventually attracted shady personalities and germinated trouble. Much of the hope for the future of Prescott was entrusted to Dodson. For thirteen years, Prescottonians and Whiskey Row regulars stood behind him like schoolchildren do with their teacher who shields them from playground bullies.[120]

James Dodson served as deputy sheriff, city marshal or chief of police (these last two terms were sometimes synonymous) and even tax collector from 1877 through 1890. He had a pedigree and résumé about which writers of frontier history dream. For starters he was the great-grandson of folk hero Daniel Boone. Dodson grew up in Clayton County, Missouri, and was the childhood friend of future outlaw icons Frank and Jesse James. With the James boys, he joined Quantrill's Raiders, riding and bushwhacking with them along the Missouri-Kansas border for two years during the Civil War. Dodson told a close friend that the sawed-off .45 Colt revolver he carried while fulfilling his duties in Prescott was a present from Jesse James's sister, Susan, given to her to tote in her dress pocket for protection. On his belt was a silver-sheathed, pearl-handled Bowie knife. Dodson used both articles on more than one occasion along Whiskey Row.[121]

One of the more amusing and early Dodson stories occurred in August 1879 when a theater troupe came to town and performed in the Prescott Theater. While watching from the green room, Dodson listened to an actor making a burlesque speech, which contained some words he felt were abusive to the U.S. Constitution. Dodson "rushed out, arrested the orator, seized him by the throat, turned him around and booted him off the stage."[122]

The Old West of the 1870s and '80s was a time when chiefs of police, sheriffs and marshals didn't delegate deputies to quell situations threatening the peace while they remained out of harm's way. They went to the scene themselves and often alone. Dodson was a representative of the latter course of action; he was often a one-man law enforcement agency. In March 1880, Dodson was called to break up a brawl behind Jackson & Tompkins' Saloon between two Chinamen—one said to have an "unpronounceable name," at least to the Caucasian tongue. Dodson used a shovel to subjugate and arrest both. One of the men, Ah Fun, was "a desperado of the highbinder type" from Los Angeles. Highbinders were a secret Chinese society, mafia-like in that they were involved in criminal activities such as prostitution and blackmail. Some were hired assassins. Ah Fun was sentenced to fifty days in jail; it was hoped this would "deter future lawlessness among his compatriots." It should be noted that Dodson, during a time when anti-Chinese sentiment was blatantly common throughout the West, protected the Chinese as vigorously as those of his own race. If he'd ever known fear or prejudice in his life, he certainly overcame them when he served in Prescott.[123]

By 1881, Dodson was the hero of Prescott and the source of stories of gallantry and triumph people loved to hear. In late November of that year, Dodson was seen walking Prescott's streets with his hand in a bandage. Upon seeing this, a zealous young *Miner* reporter ran up to him asking how he'd come to be injured. Was it inflicted during a clash with a gang of "cowboys" as he took them down one by one? Hoping to get material for an exciting article, the fledgling reporter was chagrined to learn that the cut on Dodson's hand came by a clumsy accident: "such is the fate of a poor orphan struggling to make his mark in the journalistic world."[124]

This episode occurred seven months after another entertaining arrest. In 1881, two "pistol engineers" from outside of town came to Prescott and began bar-hopping along Whiskey Row, filling up "with Prescott whisky." At one point, one of them desired to show himself Buffalo Bill Cody's equal and invited standers-by to follow him to the Plaza, where he would exhibit his skills with a six-shooter and prove there was no law officer in Prescott capable of arresting him. During the demonstration, his pistol went off, the bullet barely missing the drunken showoff's own head. The embarrassed Buffalo Bill wannabe suddenly became "as docile as a pet cow." Dodson arrested the drunken outsider using little exertion. His partner headed for the mountains and never came back.[125]

Two months later, in July 1881, one of Dodson's more spectacular arrests occurred. John Quincy Murphy of the Tip-Top mine was in town looking for a good time, if not to raise hell. Murphy was a formidable physical specimen, and a bully. Around one o'clock one mid-July morning, Murphy became unruly and then uncontrollable in an undisclosed Whiskey Row saloon. Mr. Reaves, the night watchman, was called in to placate and arrest the belligerent, but Murphy proved too much to handle. The last resort was to waken the chief of police. Dodson dressed and brought with him his celebrated Bowie knife, leaving his .45 Colt revolver behind. Once in the saloon, he ordered Murphy to quietly surrender. Murphy answered by delivering a severe blow with his fist to Dodson's temple. Dodson, not prone to turn the other temple, drew his knife and, over the course of a few minutes, deftly "inflicted upon Murphy thirteen severe but not dangerous cuts." Murphy was subdued, arrested and sent to the hospital. Dodson "surrendered himself to authorities, for examination." Prescott and Whiskey Row, however, wouldn't forsake its protector. His actions were not only called self-defense by Justice of the Peace Noyes but they also earned him a new reverence in a town that cherished law and order. The man who'd ridden with Jesse James was making frontier, law-enforcement history on Whiskey Row right before their eyes.[126]

In early 1882, after making "Prescott one of the most orderly towns on the Pacific coast," some townsfolk campaigned to raise his salary to $150 a month for fear another town (like Flagstaff) would lobby for his services. Like other efficient lawmen throughout history, however, some complained he sometimes "used too much violence, or stick, in making arrests." Nevertheless, the campaign was successful. Dodson's salary was increased. This "[p]rompt action saves to the City its good name," reported the *Miner*.[127]

Dodson quickly proved his salary raise was well deserved. In April 1882, there was a "disreputable character" named Joseph Banks in town who was spending his days in the Keg Saloon, sited on South Montezuma Street between Goodwin and Carleton Streets. One afternoon, Banks began intimidating patrons and declaring himself the new champion in town; he threatened to put anyone in a coffin who dared to arrest him. One of the owners was John "Captain" Boyd, who has often been cited as the original locator of the famous United Verde Mine of Jerome. Before it opened, the Keg Saloon was a local curiosity. Passersby couldn't help but look into the building's windows. Inside were no accoutrements that reminded anyone of a saloon. What they saw instead was a room full of kegs. But now there was trouble in the newly opened bar. Boyd tried to stop Banks, but then Banks drew his Bowie knife and threatened to carve up Boyd. This sent Boyd to the streets to find Dodson. Banks, in the meantime, stumbled over to west Prescott, where Dodson tracked him down. After Dodson submitted the obligatory order to surrender quietly, Banks's response was to throw rocks at him and call him the worst names that came to his drunken mind. At that, Dodson pulled out his own Bowie knife and gave Banks one more chance to surrender. Banks instead lunged at Dodson. This time, Dodson felt that a knife fight was a waste of time, so he quickly drew his Colt and emptied it into Banks's body. No inquiries were made. All believed the killing was completely justified, especially after it was learned who Banks was. His list of crimes included some that had recently transpired in Yavapai County, but he was also wanted for killing a man in Leadville, Colorado, and that was after he'd built a reputation as "a notorious highwayman in Illinois." All in all, it was deemed that Banks "didn't get his just deserts a moment too soon."[128]

During a mid-April 1885 evening when "[o]ld Montezuma street was alive with people," Dodson's value to Whiskey Row was once again validated:

"Chief of Police rushed in among a crowd of warriors from the country, who were playing Russians and Afghans." Picking out one individual who may've been especially disruptive, Dodson decisively disarmed and arrested him. This action had a ripple effect, which ended the row. Dodson's position earned him a salary, but his bonuses were based on commission: 10 percent of every fine connected to his arrests. In this particular arrest, the captured was fined twenty-five dollars, 10 percent of which was awarded as extra pay for Dodson.[129]

When he was reelected in 1886, bad guys were warned that if they had any hope of doing so "to give up all idea of 'running the town' this year." Prescott became a tamed town—tamed by Dodson, who truly would've been a suitable subject for a late 1950s/early '60s TV western, whose many exploits were actually not fictitious. Dodson, however, was viewed by Prescottonians as the guardian of Prescott in more ways than one. He oversaw prisoners and was often seen behind Whiskey Row "dodging around back alleys and other out of the way places, seeing that live coals, hot ashes and other substances capable of firing the town, are not scattered around promiscuously." Dodson would see more than one destructive conflagration during his time serving Prescott and play a major role in fighting them. Time after time, less dramatic reports appeared in the local newspapers, like that of Dodson "harvesting a large crop of drunks" or arresting an "inebriated biped" or some fellows who were "endeavoring to dry a few of our whisky mines." In 1878, he arrested the same woman seven times for drunken and obscene behavior. Dodson even took care of stray dog problems and delivered insane individuals to the asylum in Stockton, California.[130]

James Dodson was thirty-five years old when he began his law enforcement career in Prescott and forty-eight when he left that profoundly palpable stage. He was finally defeated in 1891, losing a reelection bid for chief of police. The *Courier* lamented, "Well; he's beaten at last. [H]e knew not fear when in defense of the lives and property of citizens." Dodson later worked as a guard at the Yuma Territorial Prison before moving to Phoenix, where he lived out his last ten years of life. Toward the end, he went into the saloon business for himself and lived in the one-hundred-room Commercial Hotel on Jefferson and Center Streets. On May 10, 1907, he was found dead sitting in a chair in the reading room of that hotel. He was sixty-four years old. On the way from Phoenix to Chicago, his casketed body was brought to Prescott. Many came to pay respect to the man who'd made their town one of the safest in the Southwest. Today, his absence in the Valhalla of Southwest heroes continues; in fact, James Dodson's name is known to very few Arizonans and a mere handful of Prescottonians. He deserves more.[131]

Returning to the early 1880s when the Dodson era was just as alive as the man himself, several events transpired that altered the landscape of Whiskey Row.

Chapter 8

Ellis and Whitney's Palace Saloon and the Whiskey Row Fire of 1883

Throughout the late 1870s and early '80s, Prescottonians were concerned that the absence of a first-class hotel kept visitors, especially visiting capitalists, from coming into town. To be a "leading town," it was thought, a first-class hotel was a must. On a near weekly basis, a plea was found in the local papers to build a hotel that would reflect the growing prosperity of Prescott. Sometimes it was accompanied by an argument, such as, "We will venture the assertion that there cannot be found in the United States a town with the number of inhabitants that Prescott has from two to three thousand without a hotel, while many have two or three." Every now and then, a hopeful would appear. The Williams House came along in 1877 and quickly began touting itself as "the only first class hotel in town." Still the entreaties came: "Night after night strangers in Prescott are turned away from our various lodging houses for lack of room."[132]

It was true. There were plenty of "lodging houses" in town, such as the Bit Saloon and Lodging House (later the Union Saloon and Lodging House) on the corner of Granite and Goodwin Streets. Its ads highlighted beds rather than rooms, for rent for twenty-five or fifty cents. The problem there was that these inexpensive rentals were designed to be utilized in tiny rooms called "cribs" for more transitory purposes other than sleeping; they were used by male "consumers" who paid for services administered by females of a certain specialized profession. Then there were establishments like Dan Hatz's Pioneer Hotel and Bakery, where a visitor could get a room for a week for eight dollars. The number of rooms in these types of places, however, was limited and often already taken, sometimes by long-term boarders. Something bigger and better was needed. The quandary seemed finally solved in April 1883 when the Sherman House opened on the south end of the plaza on Goodwin Street. Moses Hazeltine Sherman, a New Hampshire man who'd arrived in Prescott in 1872, proved the long sought after capitalist who'd open that long sought after first-class hotel. In fact, he was about to open a whole "block," a section of associated businesses whereby he would be its namesake.[133]

Immediately, citizens viewed the Sherman House as something different and "expressed delight at beholding so good a hotel in this frontier town." Attached next door to the east was a clothing store, owned by the dandy clothier Joe W. Wilson. There was another desired addition for the Sherman Block. There should be a first-class saloon, and there was an available lot next to the clothing store. Nathan Ellis and Al Whitney had seen this all coming. Enigmatically, these two were the newest proprietors of the Diana Saloon, which was still thriving. In fact, the two entrepreneurs had made many improvements to the Diana, including a lunch stand and club rooms, and the upstairs was no longer used for the meeting of fraternal organizations but was now an expansion of the billiard room. Yet they saw an opportunity they couldn't shy away from, an opportunity to create something bigger and more elegant and perhaps even become the next epicenter of Whiskey Row. The Sherman House would surely attract a new breed of clientele. A full-blown saloon in this location would be the most accessible to this fresh brand of people, which could prove a novel draw in itself.[134]

Ellis was the spokesman for this new venture. The public watched as the newest resort went up and hoped it would be an upgrade over the Whiskey Row saloons it had become proud of and whose shoulders it would stand on. As it neared completion, however, it was already missing a key ingredient. The *Courier's* expression of this would prove incredibly prophetic: "N. Ellis says that he will make [his new saloon] both useful and ornamental and yet we sigh for a stone or brick structure." Ellis responded by pointing out that all the other business owners, new and old, still used lumber for their houses. When they switched to brick, he said, he would too.[135]

On June 23, 1883, the Sherman Block's newest addition opened in grand style: "Ellis & Whitney's new saloon was formally opened Saturday evening by the breaking of a bottle of champagne, christening the place, 'The Palace.'" From descriptions provided by opening night attendees, the Palace befitted its name. It was believed to now be the largest saloon in northern Arizona Territory and in elegance superior to anything that

Ellis & Whitney's Palace Saloon can be seen here on Goodwin Street immediately to the left of J.W. Wilson's clothing store. *Sharlot Hall Museum.*

could be found in the entire Southwest. The interior radiated shameless ostentation. The walls were adorned with gold-colored paper and speckled with multifarious oil paintings depicting various natural landscapes. There was a reading room and a club room, both ornately furnished. Billiard tables were a staple in frontier resort saloons, but Ellis and Whitney upped the ante by installing three toward the back. The exterior wasn't palatial in appearance, but once inside, locals did indeed feel as if they were inside a "veritable palace." The Palace also had two of the best mixologists in Prescott in Julian Piercy (who at one time ran Thorne's Cabinet restaurant) and George Vogt. By August, it was being called the finest saloon in not only Prescott but also all of Arizona Territory.[136]

The opening of Ellis and Whitney's Palace Saloon completes the puzzle regarding the origins of today's Palace Restaurant and Saloon. There were two other "Palace" saloons that have interfered with that end. In August 1877, Gilman Shaw and Wiley Standefer—U.S. marshal of Arizona Territory at the time—took over the old Antelope Restaurant building on 112 Gurley Street. Their plan was to transform it into a first-class saloon. On September 21, 1877, it was announced that their project was finished: "Mess'rs Shaw & Standefer have fitted up the Palace Saloon in the most superb style, and filled it with choice liquors of every conceivable kind." For many years, this report has been used to date the birth year of today's Palace at 1877. Deeper research, however, proves that Shaw and Standefer's Palace Saloon—although Prescott's first "Palace"— has no connection whatsoever to the Palace presently on Montezuma Street. The 1877 Palace Saloon was a brief undertaking that was replaced by a boot and shoe store in 1878. In January 1882, another snarl was thrown into the riddle. A one-time advertisement appeared in the *Miner* announcing the opening of the "New Palace Saloon" next to Jackson & Tompkins' on Montezuma Street. Adding to the oddity, this ad heralded that it was being run by a Mrs. McManus. This was the first time a female was listed as the proprietor of a Whiskey Row saloon. This Palace Saloon appeared in print only once more, but Mrs. McManus wasn't at the helm. Describing one particular night on Whiskey Row, the *Courier* wrote, "P.M. Fisher was running the Palace and raking in coin." This was Captain "P.M." Fisher who'd later gain fame as the proprietor of Cob Web Hall. Fifteen months later, Ellis and Whitney's Palace opened on Goodwin Street. Of the three that showcased the handle "Palace Saloon," it is the first to fall in line leading to the post–Great Fire Palace Saloon still standing as the Palace Restaurant and Saloon on the twenty-first-century's Whiskey Row.[137]

Ellis and Whitney's Palace Saloon immediately drew large crowds on a nightly basis. It was the new trend-setting resort that now made all others play "catch-up," including the Cabinet and their own Diana Saloon. Two weeks later, it wouldn't matter. A stunning turn of events occurring on July 6, 1883, would radically alter Whiskey Row history and the saloon hierarchy.

THE "WHISKY ROW" FIRE OF 1883

It had rained almost the entire night of July 5, 1883, and well into the early morning of July 6. That would prove beneficial later but not at the onset of a calamity that would turn a page in Whiskey Row's young history. Morning activities had barely gotten underway when, around 8:30, the courthouse bell sounded, alerting Prescott's volunteer firemen. Fire! It would grow into the "the most destructive fire that has ever been Prescott's misfortune to experience" in its nineteen-year existence.

Soon after the bell sounded, a cannon boom was heard north of town. It came from Fort Whipple. More help was on its way as the army's hook and ladder truck hastened toward the smoke. Citizens sprinted from every direction toward the Cabinet Saloon on 118 Montezuma Street. Voluminous smoke gushed from the windows and doors of the Cabinet's restaurant section, located in the rear. "Fire, like the Apaches, comes when least expected," noted the *Courier* the next day. Within minutes, flames burst through the restaurant's rooftop, and soon the Cabinet Saloon itself. A defective flue connected to the Cabinet kitchen was the cause of the trouble.

Intensification and momentum proved an easy task for this fire. Adverse factors against fire prevention and now firefighting added up to a formidable sum. First, like modern-day strip malls, the businesses of Whiskey Row were attached to one another, creating a lengthy chain of buildings almost as if it was one long house of many rooms. Second, in the Prescott of 1883, many of the wooden edifices on Whiskey Row were relatively old, and those on middle Montezuma Street were some of the oldest in town. Most dated all the way back to 1865–66. The building that housed the Cabinet was probably of such vintage; evidence points to it being built in 1866. Up the street, the Diana was standing from untreated lumber at least fifteen years old.

Prescott's "city hose cart" arrived promptly. Ample streams of water were applied to the mounting flames. Now, however, flame and smoke were not only shooting up from the roof of the Cabinet but also issuing from the eaves of the adjoining buildings. The decaying lumber framing the buildings on middle Montezuma was providing infectious fuel for the ravenous blaze. The water's power to stifle the blaze proved no match. Almost every fire in Prescott's history has felt the influence of prevailing southerly winds. On this day, however, there was an unusual preponderant calm. The fire was traveling both north and south. Its ferocity was multiplying in both directions.

Still, the chief worry was the fire's northward path, which seemed more determined. Up Montezuma the fire crept. The Cabinet burned to the ground. The old Montezuma Saloon two doors north met the same fate, as did the Arcade Brewery. Fred Hubbard's cigar shop, J.L. Fisher's auction store and Bones & Spencer's fruit store were destroyed. Next in line was Ellis and Whitney's Diana Saloon. Firefighters were now forced to exercise foresight; the town as a whole had to be considered. If the Diana ignited there would be a danger of the inferno jumping Gurley Street. The Kelly and Stephen's store across the street was replete with flammable material—clothing and furniture, cigars, other tobacco products, stationery and newspapers. If it caught fire, a chain reaction was likely and the whole block would be in peril and perhaps more—there was a fear of the flames "taking the town." Employees and firefighters began to empty the store and saturate carpets and blankets with water. Just in case, Cotesworth Head, owner of the mercantile store on the northeast corner of Gurley and Montezuma, began preventive measures. He gave orders to dismantle the wooden balcony wrapped around his store.

The heat had become so intense, however, it was believed by most that these preventive measures would only lessen the damages should the fire cross Gurley Street. Was there a way to confine the fire to Montezuma Street? Was blowing up the Diana the only hope of stopping the fire in its tracks? A quick decision was needed. Although there was some debate, a quick one was made. Since the Diana was surely doomed, the choice was clear. John Kirwagen, a cattle rancher, volunteered to do the dirty work. Rushing to beat the fire before it devoured the saloon, citizens ran into the Diana to remove "fixtures and chattels." In the meantime, Kirwagen placed fifty pounds of "giant powder"—nitroglycerin and kieselguhr—underneath the Diana's steps. The explosion was set off. Observers were amazed at how perfectly the rancher's efforts had worked. The Diana toppled quietly to the ground in a massive heap, which firefighters instantly splattered with water. The conflagration's northward march had been arrested.

The southward movement of the fire would find its deterrent already in place. John Greenway Campbell had been operating the town's most active mercantile store on mid-Montezuma Street since 1866. As ambitious as early Prescott's early entrepreneurs were, the "ever-advancing" Campbell seemed more so and acted with more foresight. Along with William Buffum, he had built one of Prescott's first stone and brick buildings, the first so-called fireproof structure on Whiskey Row. Before the wooden "mammoth" Diana Saloon was erected in 1868, the Campbell and Buffum mercantile store was the pride of Prescott and the model future builders were encouraged to emulate: "Their large fire-proof stone store, with brick front, is the finest building in town, and is inferior to no building this side of Los Angeles." It would prove priceless that morning and support the argument, better than mere words could ever do, that there was a need for more stone and brick buildings.

Campbell's store stood on lots 22 and 23, addresses 124–126 Montezuma Street. He had also installed iron shutters in the front that resisted the flames.

For once, wood wasn't present as the ally of fire. Stone and brick proved worthy opponents against Prescott's worst fear. A bucket brigade formed in front of the store—the water coming from a plaza well—which assisted the streams coming from hoses. Flame eventually fed on flame only. The fire had met its match. The southward advance of the fire was stopped with the help of a stone and brick building standing in the gap. John Campbell's preventive measure had paid off; the lower half of Whiskey Row was saved. The value of brick had been undoubtedly proven.[138]

The northern half of Whiskey Row became the "burnt out district" for several months. It had a surprise coming its way, and its effect is still in place today.

Chapter 9

The Whiskey Row of Montezuma Street Takes Shape

With almost half of the Montezuma Street section of Whiskey Row in ashes, Ellis and Whitney's new Palace Saloon had no legitimate competition. Gone were the Cabinet and their own Diana Saloon. Prescott and its visitors would have to rely more heavily on the "much admired" Palace for its kind of recreation. Although busier than ever, the next six months were peaceful at the Palace. The Sazerac Saloon on Gurley Street picked up some extra business. A new saloon, opened by Sport Boyle, cropped up on the southern end of Montezuma. It would take the place of the Parlor. It was called Cob Web Hall, which later became perhaps the most famous pre–Great Fire Whiskey Row saloon, ironically, for an affair that never occurred there. That story, which became a remarkable legend, is reserved for another chapter. In 1883, the Arcade Brewery was rebuilt, and next to it rose the Eclipse Saloon on 106 Montezuma Street. It would be run by a man who owned the name probably most familiar to those interested in Palace Saloon history, Robert Brow. During the Eclipse's opening night, by 9:00 p.m. the enthused Brow "had already burst two buttons off his vest, drinking." Brow would advertise his saloon by asking, "HAVE YOU SEEN the Eclipse?" D.C. Thorne, who chose not to rebuild the Cabinet immediately, took it over in October 1884. Thorne immediately made the Eclipse Montezuma Street's most popular saloon. He drew such a crowd on its reopening night that he quickly closed it to add an annex. Something went wrong, however, along the way. The Eclipse would prove Thorne's only failure at the saloon business. It was shut down in 1885. In May, Joe Wilson moved his clothing store there. Thorne's thoughts returned to rebuilding the Cabinet Saloon.[139]

Before the Eclipse closed, however, another catastrophe ensued that would change Whiskey Row forever.

THE SHERMAN BLOCK FIRE OF 1884

With much of the Montezuma Street portion of Whiskey Row still bare or being rebuilt, when the fire alarm bell sounded in the very early morning of Valentine's Day 1884, a literal nightmare had already begun. A sense of "This cannot be happening again" struck Prescottonians like a lightning bolt. Within minutes, three-fourths of the populace had rushed toward the Sherman House, already overwhelmed by flames and deemed doomed. The *Miner* described the early stages of the Sherman House fire in savagely poetic language: "Along the wooden and papered walls the forked tongues of fire leaped and chased each other with demonized and resistless fury." Fortunately, hotel guests were warned at the fire's onset and "barely escaped with their lives."

By the time help arrived, the structures on each side and behind the Sherman House were in jeopardy. In between the Sherman House and the Palace, the contents inside Wilson's clothing store made that building most flammable. The rapidity in which it went up in flames was coupled by a gentle wind blowing in from the southwest. That left the Palace helpless. Two men were inside it when the alarm bell sounded, Al Whitney and Julian Piercy. With some assistance, they were able to pull out the entire bar, one billiard table and a piano before the Palace was engulfed. Several buildings next to and behind the Sherman House also succumbed to flames.

Now the entire block was in danger. Remembering how well dynamiting had worked during the Montezuma Street fire of 1883, it was thought this would be the only way to save it. Police chief James Dodson took charge, as was his nature. Thinking and moving quickly, he and his assistants first blew up a paint store and then J.L. Fisher's store house on the corner of Goodwin and Montezuma. It worked, and "the limits of the fire had been fixed and its further spreading made impossible."

After the conflagration and chaos were quelled, a terrible rumor began spreading. The owner and editor of the *Miner*, Samuel Nelson Holmes, was missing. He and his wife had been staying in a suite in the northwest corner of the Sherman House, near where the fire was thought to have started due to a defective flue, like the 1883 fire. It was believed that Mrs. Holmes was perhaps the first to spot the fire and that she bravely went from room to room to warn guests to save themselves. She'd been the one most responsible for saving those in the hotel. Her reward was tragic. Mr. Holmes was apparently somewhere else in the hotel when the crisis began. Upon hearing the alarm bell, it was believed that he ran back to his room to save his wife and perhaps grab some valuable papers. The dark morning yielded to the sunrise. When the ruins of the Sherman House had cooled enough to be searched, a charred body was found, a "scarcely recognizable remains of a human being." Holmes was the only one known to have still been in the hotel when it burned. Later a shirtsleeve's studs and buttons were identified as his, and his friends' and families' fears were confirmed.[140]

THE PALACE SALOON MOVES TO MONTEZUMA STREET

With much of Block 13's Montezuma Street's businesses still being rebuilt and now Goodwin Street's Sherman Block razed by flames, Prescott had an opportunity. This was perhaps the third most important time in Whiskey Row's history, the first being its birth in 1864 and the second after the Great Fire of 1900. The year 1884 saw Whiskey Row at a crossroads. Would it be rebuilt, and where?

Gone were Prescott's largest hotel and the Palace, "the handsomest, best fitted bar and billiard saloon in Northern Arizona." As in 1883, the call arose again for brick buildings. There were no "I told you sos" from the *Miner* or *Courier*, although they would've been merited. The *Courier* especially had reason to smirk, which had told Ellis and Whitney that as wonderful as their Palace was, "yet we sigh for a stone or brick structure." Two destructive fires within six months of each other caused Prescottonians to think harder about the physical fabric of their town. The death of *Miner* editor Samuel Nelson snapped some into a new reality. In March 1884, it was announced that "Montezuma Street will shortly loom up with several fine brick buildings." Ellis and Whitney, however, weren't yet sure if they wanted to rebuild. Within a span of seven months, they had lost two of the best saloons Prescott had ever known, the Diana and the Palace. They had lost $8,000 in the Palace fire and got $5,000 back from insurance. For many, the Palace had been such a positive addition to Prescott, it was hoped that its once proud owners would "shortly secure a good business location and start again, to grow up with the country." Ellis and Whitney announced in late March their plans to reopen on Montezuma Street. When they did, the location was one the Palace would never leave.[141]

What better night to open a palace than the evening of July 4? It was estimated that some one thousand people attended to see the new eighty-by twenty-five-foot Palace Saloon now standing where D.C. Thorne's Cabinet Saloon had operated for nine years, on lot 19, 118 Montezuma Street. A band played outside to make it known this was no small event. For the time being, the bar that was pulled out onto Goodwin Street was used while Frank Parker constructed a new twenty-foot bar made of solid walnut. Three gaming tables were installed nearby. As one entered the saloon, on the right was a ten- by twenty-foot reading room with French plate mirrors hung on each wall. It was filled with periodicals and newspapers from all over the country. In the main room were lamps and chandeliers that lit up the walls, which were covered with wine-tinted paper. In the rear was heard a trio of Prescott musicians: Ed Long on piano, H.T. Martin on violin and S.B. Swidensky on the cornet. George Vogt and Julian Piercy were still spinning their magic behind the bar. Most importantly, every measure was finally taken to safeguard against fire: a stone foundation, brick walls and iron roofs and shutters.[142]

As attractive as it was, it didn't take long for ugliness to befall the Palace.

MURDER IN THE PALACE

Two months after the new Palace opened, it was baptized with a brutal crime. The *Courier* called it Dickensian. Fred Glover, a former bouncer at the Diana Saloon who later became "a dissolute gambler and an irreclaimable opium fiend," brutally killed his lover there. Glover had been working at the Sazerac Saloon but had also become financially dependent on his lover, Jennie Clark. Clark, whose real name was Nellie Coyle, was a prostitute. She was described as "a comely woman of not more than 26 years old, of frail and delicate frame." Although deemed a "social outcast," it was thought she'd been raised in a more genteel environment because her behavior had some refinement to it. She was also sick with consumption and perhaps even on the verge of dying. Clark and thirty-something Glover lived together on Granite Street in an apartment at Madame Mamie Pearson's bordello.

After getting off earlier than expected at the Sazerac on August 28, rather than going home, Glover decided to head around the corner to Prescott's current hot spot, the Palace. Reports implied that Glover didn't go home right away because he was angry that, earlier in the day, he had entreated Jennie to give him $100 but she refused. Half past midnight, Jennie decided to look for him, so she grabbed her best friend, Dora Palmer. They crossed Whiskey Row Alley, walked straight into the Palace and coaxed him to come home. As the two lovers prepared for bed, Jennie saw how sloshed Glover was and, to Glover's displeasure, decided it was her turn to have some fun. She and Dora headed back to the Palace and began drinking—heavily, according to witnesses. Glover, in the meantime, decided to do some bar-hopping on his own. By the time he arrived back at the Palace, he was even more intoxicated. He'd brought two acquaintances, Jim Carruthers and a Mr. Harris. When they walked in, there on the music stand was Jennie, singing her heart out with Dora accompanying her on the piano. Glover, with help from Harris, immediately heckled Jennie, which caused her to cry out, "Damn it, you needn't make fun of me!" Glover and his friends moved to the end of the Palace's walnut bar and invited Jennie and Dora to join them. Jennie's response was, "No, I won't drink with a damned son of a bitch." Witnesses weren't sure if she'd directed this comment at Glover or Harris. Soon after, however, Jennie and Harris were exchanging insults and vulgarities, Jennie giving as well as she was taking. Instead of supporting his girlfriend, Glover defended Harris, telling her she was being too harsh.

Soon Jennie and Glover were in each other's faces. Someone pushed first, maybe Jennie, but it was she who wound up on the Palace floor. Bartenders Piercy and Vogt stepped in, and Jennie took refuge behind the bar. While there, she grabbed a bottle of soda water and hurled it toward Glover and Harris. Glover fired back by missiling several bar glasses at her. Somehow the bartenders were able to gain temporary control. When Jennie returned to the end of the bar and put her hand to her head, she discovered one bar glass had caused a gash. She screamed, "My God, my head!" More insults flew back and forth between Jennie and the two men, so Glover knocked her to the floor again. Jennie cried for help, but this time no one came to her aid. There was a man named John Ellis present who was running for sheriff. He was criticized later for not stepping in while a woman was getting beaten.

Jennie was able to get up. She then turned her venom on Harris, who reacted by knocking her to the floor for a third time. This time Glover actually helped her up. He walked her over to the south wall to continue their argument in imagined privacy, but both were too drunk and too angry. Jennie bawled that she'd never love Glover again because he hadn't defended her against Harris, especially after she'd supported him financially and even after his friends had deserted him. As those words came out of her mouth she became more enraged with every remembrance. Jennie shrieked, "Damn you, strike me if you dare!" then hit Glover in the face. Glover swung back, connecting and knocking her to the floor for the fourth and last time. After shouting, "Damn you, let's see how you faint now, and do it pretty!" he started kicking the fragile Jennie, stomping her repeatedly in the head, neck and chest. Jim Carruthers finally intervened, hollering, "Damn it, my mother was a woman and I can't stand seeing a woman stamped!" He and another pulled Jennie away from her attacker, but she appeared to be unconscious. Somehow she was taken home, apparently with Glover's help. Fifteen minutes later, around three o'clock that Friday morning, Jennie Clark died.

Glover was suddenly overwhelmed with remorse; he wept over his lover's dead body, hugging and holding her. He then sprinted over to James Dodson's house and woke him and desperately explained that he was being accused of killing Jennie but was innocent. Dodson calmed him and told him to go home. He would look into it. Glover instead returned to the Palace. After seeing Jennie dead in her apartment, Dodson found Glover and arrested him. After word spread that a woman had been beaten to death, a call for a lynching went out. Wiser minds prevailed. The *Courier* admonished that surely, a fair trial would be held and "the hangman's services will be again necessary to purify the moral atmosphere and vindicate the outraged majority."[143]

Jenny Clark was buried in an unmarked grave the next day in the Citizens Cemetery. Glover had requested to attend but was denied. He wept in jail the entire day. Only a few women followed her casket to the cemetery, all of her profession. It didn't take long for Glover to be tried and sentenced to hang for first-degree murder. A successful appeal to Governor Frederick Tritle reduced his sentence to life imprisonment. The next year, Governor Meyer Zulick granted clemency; now he was to serve only ten years. Things continued to get better for Glover. In 1890, Governor Nathan Oakes Murphy pardoned him. He was released on December 20, 1890. In mid-January 1891, he was seen once more in Prescott. Fred Glover was en route to Seattle and never heard from again.[144]

THE NEW WHISKEY ROW

In 1885, Nathan Ellis was elected to Congress, so Al Whitney ran the Palace solo. This may have proved too much. It was closed for a spell before Theodore Eggars took over. His plan was to reopen in late July, which he did. What happened then is a mystery. An announcement was made that on September 18 the Palace would "be re-opened in a couple of weeks by a Californian" named J.J. Gunn. Gunn's debut was on Saturday October 3, and "Prescott was herself again." Once again, the Palace was recognized as the finest resort in the land. Gunn brought the Palace's popularity to new heights. A singer was added to its musical offerings. In fact, the music was of such quality that it was soon considered the Palace's main draw. On that opening night, it was only one of the saloons packed with patrons. Whiskey Row was alive once more, as the Sazerac, Cob Web, Headquarters, Maier's, Bit and Little Diana saloons received their fair share of business. The Little Diana was built in 1883 by W.D. Black and C.T. Lewis. It replaced the old Diana until the Burke Hotel grabbed the corner of Montezuma and Gurley Streets in 1891 and kept it.[145]

On September 30, 1886, D.C. Thorne and Pete Kastner, "at great expense," reopened the Cabinet Saloon. It featured a beautiful bar of black

Today, Hotel St. Michael, originally the Burke Hotel, stands on the corner where the Diana Saloon made Whiskey Row history from 1868 to 1883. *Norman Fisk.*

walnut and cherry. Nineteen feet of mirrors, elegantly framed, were behind it. Thorne and Kastner also installed a music stand and lunch counter. In the rear, they opened another Cabinet Chop House, which offered "all the delicacies of the season."[146]

The Palace experienced several proprietary changes. In 1887, Charles Morgan ran it. By April of the next year, it was leased to Thorne, who had sold his half proprietorship of the Cabinet to Kastner. Rather than proprietor, Thorne called himself the Palace's "manager." Because of its prominence on Whiskey Row today, the Palace has absorbed several legends. One of Arizona's most popular ones, the legend of "Kissin' Jenny," is sometimes said to have transpired partly in the Palace during Thorne's three-year shift there. It's the tale of how Prescott lost the capital to Phoenix in 1889. Longtime Arizona senator Barry Goldwater, who once lamented, "My only regret is that I didn't buy the Palace when I had a chance," recounted this story to his friend, Tom Sullivan, who was trying to purchase that saloon in 1977: "The story is that the leader of the Senate, having one glass eye and who frequented the [Palace], had his glass eye stolen. As a result, he couldn't take his place in the Territorial Senate and the lack of his vote sent the capital to Phoenix." It was said that this vainglorious scoundrel, representing Yavapai County and therefore Prescott, had a favorite prostitute working out of the Palace, Kissin' Jenny. She, so the legend goes, was thus hired by some chicanerous Maricopa County politicians to steal the fake eye if possible. They knew this delegate's vanity would prevent him from attending the voting session scheduled the next day, even with the issue of the territorial capital at stake; it was anticipated the vote would be close. Sure enough, when the delegate awoke the next morning, the eye, which he'd placed in a glass of water on a bed stand, was gone. Jenny told the politician that she'd gotten thirsty during the night and drank the water down along with the fake eye. This kept him from leaving her boudoir, and his missing vote permanently sent the capital to Phoenix.[147]

Did anything like this happen? It's a marvelous story and something like it might've happened; there is even evidence suggesting that Thorne's wife, Mary, operated a boardinghouse that sponsored prostitution somewhere on Montezuma Street. Even if Kissin' Jenny worked there, however, she isn't to blame for the capital being located in Phoenix rather than Prescott. Some stubborn facts get in the way. Legislative Act No. 1 was signed by Governor Zulick on January 26, 1889, which moved the capital to Phoenix. The vote passed by seven votes and "was railroaded through both houses at the rate of sixty miles an hour." The only councilman absent was from Apache County.

Lot 20 on Montezuma Street was often used jointly by the Palace and Cabinet saloons but today is the center section of the Palace Restaurant and Saloon. *Norman Fisk.*

He was home taking care of a sick child. All Yavapai County legislators were present for the vote.[148]

In 1892, Robert Brow bought a 50 percent interest in the Palace. His famous stint there had begun. One of his first orders of business was to expand the saloon's restaurant and menu. Eventually the Palace owned what was perhaps Prescott's most extensive menu, with full meals for twenty-five or fifty cents. Lot 20, 120 Montezuma Street, where the main section of the Palace sits today, has a varied history. After the Cabinet and Palace became near neighbors, separated by lot 20, it was used jointly by both, halved by a partition. Tonsorial parlors, bathhouses and extra dining space were some of the diverse uses for this lot. In 1892, the Cabinet closed for a spell for repairs and operated there for the time being. In 1896, the Cabinet's proprietorship was split three ways: Ben Belcher, Arthur Cordiner and Barney Smith. The Cabinet's restaurant section operated in the rear section of lot 20 and the dining room extended over onto lot 21.[149]

In the 1890s, saloons were an accepted and integral part of Prescott's life and economy. The temperance movement, however, was gaining strength throughout the country, and Prescott wasn't safe from it. More than two decades after missionaries Cedarholm and Garrison attempted to scare men sober with the threat of hell, the Salvation Army sent an advanced guard to

Arizona's most notable saloon town: two young ladies, Maude Bigney and Clara Clemo. They had obtained use of the opera house to hold services and were expected to attract large crowds because both were "handsome ladies." This they did, but several attendees were there to oppose the soldiers' cause: "Complaints have been made of rude conduct on the part of some young men who attend the meetings." Yet this attractive duo was more formidable than Whiskey Row regulars anticipated. They went to the jails and held street revivals right there on Montezuma Street. One especially memorable one was held in front of the Palace Saloon, one of their targeted "hell holes of Prescott." After the service, the pair walked boldly into the Palace and began recruiting soldiers for their cause. Most candidates therein, however, weren't willing to volunteer; "the army has not yet succeeded in enlisting many recruits," said the *Miner*. The ladies tried every strategy, even offering free meals at their new headquarters on South Montezuma Street: "As but very few have accepted the invitation the inference is there are few people in Prescott who are not able to obtain their [own] food." Even Prescott's "church people" resisted joining. Eventually, the ladies were compelled to abandon their headquarters. In its place was built a saloon built by Jerry Barton, well known throughout Arizona. The irony wasn't lost on Prescottonians or Barton. He invited Cedarholm and Garrison to his saloon's opening. Barton rendered "an ode and fir[ed] a volley at 8 p.m. sharp" for the ladies. It is doubtful the courageous pair attended.[150]

An Isolated but Notable Fire

The Palace Saloon's brick was tested Friday evening around six o'clock, November 5, 1897. This was no minor fire. "A lurid glare" was seen in the Palace from Montezuma Street. A shout of "fire" followed, as did a burst of flames from its front windows, shattering the glass and the electric light rondures. A pipe above the steak fryer in the kitchen oven had broken and ignited the fire. The fire department arrived with a "swiftness that would be worthy of emulation in many larger cities" and quickly extinguished the flames. The wooden portions of the Palace burned to a crisp; "the front end of one of the most handsomely finished and best appointed saloons in Arizona presented a charred mass of ruins while the water stood six inches on the floor." Of great significance, the solid walnut bar was destroyed and would have to be replaced. The rest of the building, made of brick, stood firm. In fact, it was thought that if the Palace hadn't been a brick structure, a repeat of the 1883 fire would've been likely. The damages were estimated at $5,000, all covered by insurance. Robert Brow began repairs immediately.[151]

The Palace didn't reopen until December 28, but when it did, it was festive. A brass band welcomed a throng that considered the new Palace a work of art: "Everything about the place betokens both elegance and taste." Some noteworthy changes were made. One, the restaurant and dining area of the Palace were moved to the rear of the building and made separate from the saloon. A back entrance was created that bypassed the saloon area so that "ladies who object to entering a saloon, may be properly served." Second, a new bar was fitted. The *Miner*'s description of it is significant: "The new bar is one of the handsomest in the south-west. It is made of cherry and is massive in proportions and finished in the most elaborate and artistic style." This surely was the Palace bar that was being used when the Great Fire of 1900 struck Whiskey Row, and its description closely matches that of the famed bar that sits in the Palace today. There is a legend that the Palace bar was pulled out to the Plaza during the Great Fire of 1900 and reinstalled in 1901. Although no absolutely conclusive evidence has yet surfaced, this

This recently rediscovered photo of the Palace Saloon interior was taken sometime between 1897 and 1900 and appears to show the bar that is still featured in the Palace today. *Sharlot Hall Museum.*

The bar seen in the Palace Restaurant and Saloon today may have been installed in 1897 and most likely survived the Great Fire of 1900. *Norman Fisk.*

description—and the bar counter seen in the image at the bottom of page 108—certainly allows for a strong possibility it is true.[152]

The 1890s were relatively peaceful on Whiskey Row. There were, however, three major events that proved unforgettable.

THE DYNAMITE DEMON OF THE CABINET SALOON

It was called "a dastardly deed" and the work of a demon. After twenty-six years of Prescott history, it was the newest atrocity without parallel. By today's standards, it would be considered a terrorist-like attack because, even though the perpetrator had targeted only one person, he was willing to kill others in the process. It was Sunday night, June 28, 1896. Without any indication that something might be amiss, an explosion detonated that was so powerful that it shook nearly all the other buildings along Whiskey Row and could be heard throughout all of Prescott. The result was the demolishment of a twenty-five-square-foot area in the Cabinet dining room, as well as damaging its neighboring businesses, the Palace barbershop and Al Dake's merchandise store.

Ten minutes before the blast, a saloon full of people were enjoying the usual delights offered by the Cabinet: gambling, a spirited drink and conversation. In the back was a restaurant run by Chinese men, which wasn't unusual on Whiskey Row. Two ladies—"habitués of Granite street," which Prescottonians knew to mean they were prostitutes—were dining at a table in the restaurant area. One was Bertha Hovey, or at least that was the name she went by. Her companion was known only as Cora. Both were presently being served by a Chinese waiter. The lives of all three were about to suddenly and dramatically change.

At about twenty minutes before ten o'clock, just beneath Bertha and Cora's feet erupted a deafening explosion. Proprietor Barney Smith jumped to his feet. One frequent patron named Tom, who'd been participating in a game of dice and was known for having rheumatism, seemed suddenly healed. He sprinted out the front door. The head chef of the Chinese kitchen immediately thought the Cabinet was being attacked by Highbinders. He howled to the heavens for help.

All inside the Cabinet were so stunned that it took some time to realize what had happened. The explosion was so thunderous that hundreds outside the enclosure hurried to the site to see what had happened. Some suspected this was all part of a robbery attempt, that the explosion was merely a planned distraction. Had robbers set off the explosion? Were they now waiting to pounce and scoop up any money on the gambling tables, blown to the floor or in the register? Frank Williams, the popular barkeep of the Cabinet, stayed near the money just in case.

Although the *Miner* reported that the blast went off at "precisely" 9:40 p.m., the *Courier* reported that the hands of the clock blown off of the saloon wall were stopped at ten minutes until ten o'clock. The damages extended into the bar area. Anything that could move in the Cabinet had been displaced. Tables and chairs were knocked flat, and glass from the windows and pieces of linoleum lay strewn everywhere. The dining room and kitchen were destroyed, as was the back porch. Most amazingly, the one-thousand-pound oven in the Cabinet kitchen had been knocked over. Damages were later estimated at $1,000, which included $300 worth of imported liquors and a new $40 chandelier that had crashed to the ground.

After everyone had gathered their wits, those involved in mining work agreed that they were enveloped in a familiar odor. Dynamite fumes filled the air. In fact, some maintained there'd been an unusual odor in the air *before* the blast. There was no doubt that the death of someone, or several, had been the intention of whoever had set off this explosion.

Incredibly, the two soiled doves and the Chinese waiter survived. One of the ladies was harmed more than the other, but it wasn't clear which: "One of the women is laid up for repairs, while the other is as yet uninjured, but the Chinese waiter has a bad wound on one of his legs." All in all, considering the magnitude of the explosion and the collateral damages it wreaked, their survival was considered a miracle. Instant death would've been the expected result. Then again, there may've been some science behind it. Someone thought about the pieces of linoleum laying all over the wreckage. It was theorized that the unusually heavy layer of linoleum covering the restaurant floor had arrested the force of the blast and spread it to other areas. In fact, neither lady had been thrown from the area in which they were sitting, and at first, neither realized that dynamite had been placed directly below them—or that one, or both, of them may have been the target.

Of course, the big questions were "Who?" and "Why?" Chief of Police Steve Prince began an investigation. After robbery was eliminated as motivation, certain facts came to light that couldn't be denied. One, whoever effected this act was familiar with the use and the power of dynamite. Evidence also began to suggest it was Bertha Hovey who had been targeted. Her "professional" colleagues mentioned to local authorities and Prince that someone had indeed been stalking Bertha and making threats. Furthermore, Bertha not only had a husband but a jealous one. His name was William Binkley, a miner who'd been working at the nearby Last Chance Mine. When questioned, Bertha, for reasons that would later surface, claimed that, no, he couldn't be the demon dynamiter, for they were "on pleasant terms." Nevertheless, suspicion ran high. Prince arrested him.[153]

At first Binkley asserted innocence, but a guilty conscience prevented him from sustaining that lie for long. On July 19, he confessed to the crime. His motive was more than disdain for Bertha's profession, if he had any at all. Soon after they were married, almost as if the whole thing had been a prank, Bertha told him she had another husband who was alive and well in Colorado. Whether Binkley and Bertha ever lived together is uncertain, but she had clearly arranged for them to live apart. Binkley confessed that he'd stalked her "at her adobe" many times. Bertha, however, would chase him off by belittling and laughing at him.

Binkley's anger grew to a boiling point; he began planning a murder/ suicide. As a mine worker, he'd become handy with "giant powder," and it was available for "free" at the Last Chance Mine. Binkley procured six sticks of dynamite with three feet of fuse and one cap from a nearby cabin there. He hid it behind the Double-Decker on Granite Street, which may have

Now part of the dining room of the Palace Saloon and Restaurant, this area is approximately where William Binkley detonated dynamite in an attempt to kill his wife in the Cabinet Saloon in 1896. *Norman Fisk.*

been Bertha's work place. On the night of June 28, he learned where Bertha was sitting in the Cabinet. Taking his explosives to the Cabinet cellar, he placed them below his wife's table, lit the fuse and fled to the Royal Saloon down the street. Thirty seconds after he entered the Royal, the massive blast was heard across town. Binkley soon returned to the scene of his crime. He later divulged that if he had seen Bertha dead, he would've followed "his mistress to the unknown." Indeed, he was carrying enough laudanum at the time to fulfill that purpose. Seeing his once-beloved alive, however, and that he hadn't supplied her with the ultimate lesson he desired to teach her, Binkley cancelled his planned self-inflicted death and walked off into the night. After confessing to the crime, he tried to persuade the police chief to arrest Bertha for bigamy. Prince refused.

Bertha most likely resumed her career as soon as she was able. Binkley was convicted and sent to the Yuma Territorial Prison. Belcher and Smith were left with the costly job of repairing the Cabinet. They were back in business in a month.[154]

THE PALACE SALOON HOLDUP OF 1898

Prescottonians seemed proud of what transpired in the early morning of January 9, 1898. "A DARING HOLD UP!" one headline screamed. That was followed with the subtitle, "A Lone Man Does a Neat Job in This Line at the Palace Saloon Sunday Morning." This report, which treated the crime like an accomplishment, started with, "One of the most clever and daring robberies which has been committed for many a day in Arizona occurred about four o'clock on Sunday morning at the Palace saloon."

Robert Brow had gone home. The crap game dealer was still at his table. The roulette wheel operator had joined him. The bartender was in the tiny office to the right of the bar. About twenty patrons were still hanging around. Just after 4:00 a.m., a heavyset man peeked through the front door and then disappeared. A few minutes later, a smaller man with his face covered in cloth charged through the door and nimbly jumped over the bar with a six-shooter held high in his right hand. Clearly pre-planned, he then pulled the bartender out of his office, placed the pistol to his head and ordered him to throw up his hands and move quickly to the craps table. At first, the bartender, taken totally by surprise, thought it was a prank and called out, "What does this mean?" Starting with a few curse words, the masked man answered, "You march over there, and I will show you what this means." The bartender complied. The roulette man was ordered to join the procession with the bartender. Keeping the six-shooter trained on the craps dealer with his right hand, the masked marauder then magically produced a canvas sack from his coat pocket with his left. He ordered the craps dealer to place all the booty—over thirty pounds worth—on the table into the bag. In went $447 worth of silver. After throwing the filled sack over his left shoulder, he backed his way to the rear door, ordered all to not move and threatened to shoot at anyone who "poked their heads out of the door." No one moved, and no one poked.

The police were notified immediately, and a hunt for the man of average height and slight build began. What was seen of his face was identified as being pale. They were also looking for the heavyset man who had glanced into the Palace before the robbery; he was thought to be the thief's scout and lookout. Neither was captured.[155]

For eight days, this daring robbery was the talk of the town. On January 17, this changed. Two short doors south, a series of events started that spawned what is perhaps Arizona's most famous saloon story and almost certainly its best. Over time, this story took an intriguing path toward legend that can be described as uniquely extraordinary.

Chapter 10

Arizona's Most Famous Saloon Story

The Legend of Chance Cobweb Hall and the True Story of Violet "Baby Bell" Hicks

There is a touching legend that's been shared for decades along Whiskey Row that speaks of a baby who was won in a gambling game after being abandoned atop a bar counter of a prominent Whiskey Row saloon. It has been featured in newspapers, magazines, books and poetry. Of the hundreds extant, it's perhaps Arizona's best and most famous saloon story. According to the popularly told story—a mostly magical, "happily ever after" tale—the baby's name was Chance Cobweb Hall. However, there was no such person, at least one who went by that name. Yet a "baby left on a bar counter" episode did occur on Whiskey Row. The baby's name was Violet Bell. She was adopted as Violet Hicks and died as Violet Binner. Although the true story has its enchanting moments, it's certainly not as glorious as the Chance Cobweb Hall legend.

The Chance Cobweb Hall legend traces back to 1927 when one of the most respected figures in Arizona Territory history, Edmund Wells, published his frontier days memoirs: *Argonaut Tales: Stories of the Gold Seekers and the Early Indian Scouts*. It has been characterized as "a colorful *first-hand* [italics added] portrayal of early days in Arizona Territory." Within it was a three-chaptered section entitled "Chance Cobweb Hall." Therein, Wells recounted in prosaic detail the story of a baby girl dropped off and abandoned on a Whiskey Row saloon counter, twenty-nine years after the actual event. It concluded, happily, with who she became as an adult and her high standing in society. Over time, through persistent retelling, his story became "history."

Edmund Wells was one of Arizona Territory's most accomplished citizens and a creator of Whiskey Row lore. *Sharlot Hall Museum.*

Why was the Chance Cobweb Hall story accepted as historical verity for more than seventy years? An original Prescottonian, Wells boasted a résumé of beyond-the-norm accomplishments several pages long. It's a record that includes being the first Republican candidate for governor after Arizona was awarded statehood and a longtime president of the Bank of Arizona, and he's widely believed to be Arizona's first millionaire. Still more crucial, Wells owned an enduring reputation of unwavering integrity. No tangible reason existed to *not* take Wells's version at face value.[156]

Wells's account assigns the setting for the initial incidents to Cob Web Hall and its ownership to the magnetic Captain "P.M." Fisher. Citing no actual date, he simply noted that it was a snowy winter night, and the

115

"Cobweb" offered a warm haven. The gambling tables had been bustling, but activity began tapering. Drinks and cigars had been sold by the gallon and bushel, but the smoke was beginning to clear. The cantina's popular female vocalist had retired for the night, as had many others. Some soldiers from Fort Whipple and miners from the nearby mountains were stretching the evening a tad longer. A few of Captain Fisher's friends remained, including two Prescott icons: Colonel Henry Bigelow and his best friend, Prescott's original surveyor, Robert Groom. They were amid the group lagging behind hoping to engage Fisher socially. It was then the tone of the night suddenly transmuted into the bizarre.

Someone noticed a peculiar bundle atop the part of the bar counter closest to the entrance, peculiar because it was moving. A sound, although stifled, was coming from it. None had seen it before now or knew how it arrived or how long it had been there. Bigelow summoned Fisher, who unraveled the parcel to discover a beautiful, ebony-eyed baby girl. He held her aloft for all to see. Although some "grizzled miners" were dumbstruck, the majority extended a hearty welcome. It didn't take long for all to comprehend that she'd been abandoned and was now homeless.

Almost instantly, arguments commenced regarding the baby's immediate and future welfare. Soldiers and miners proffered their respective cases for adoption. Dissension started to radiate throughout the saloon. Before the situation got out of control, Fisher interjected with a proposal. All desirous of adopting the child, he submitted, should partake in a game of dice: ten dollars for one throw of four dice for the pretty stranger. All money pooled would go to the winner to jump-start her long-term care. None dissented. After all, the Whiskey Row way of life embraced gambling.

Player after player rolled. Finally it came time for the most unlikely candidate for parenthood to play: the aged bachelor Robert Groom. He laid out four fives, and with that, the game seemed over. Groom declared himself the winner. However, patiently waiting his turn was Judge Charley Hall. He announced that nothing was decided yet; he had the last throw. Excitement akin to that of overtime at a sporting event filled the room as Hall braced for the roll. The dramatic moment resulted in a miraculous throw of four sixes. Hall had won the baby. Joyous congratulations and applause came from all but the suspicious Groom. Had Hall somehow loaded the dice? Groom conceded, but with one stipulation: he must name the baby. The judge consented immediately. The speech Wells attributed to Groom is worthy of being quoted in full. Lifting his glass of champagne, he toasted: "As the bead of this sparkling wine ascends to the surface, so may the destiny of this little waif rise from obscurity and sparkle amongst the stars of the heaven on earth, uplifting humanity making us better men and better women. And in memory of this presence I now christen thee, little miss, and name thee, CHANCE COBWEB HALL. Drink."

Now the judge faced the matter of telling Mrs. Hall the improbable story of how it came to pass that he was bringing a baby home for keeps. As she held the child, trepidation shook her voice when she asked her husband to explain. Her fears eased as she listened to his Whiskey Row story. When her husband finished, Mrs. Hall announced, "Let us give it the best care our meager fortune will provide." The couple agreed to adopt the baby. It was convenient that the couple's last name was "Hall" so that Groom's christening needed no surname change.

Wells maintained that several fruitless attempts were made to locate the birth parents. Nonetheless, Mrs. Hall soon learned how the baby wound up on a bar counter on Whiskey Row and who deposited her there. It was George Ah Fat, the Chinese laundry proprietor. His business registry mark had been found on one of the baby's garments, which led her to visit and quiz him. Reluctantly, Ah Fat confessed that a striking woman had left the baby in his care until she was able to better her circumstances. But after some time, he concluded she wasn't going to return and that there had to be a more appropriate place for a girl to be raised. He believed his friend, Captain Fisher, would know what to do. Instead of going directly to Fisher, however, he decided to drop her off on the counter of his saloon during a cold, stormy night and then blend into the crowd. That was all Ah Fat was willing to offer. Soon, wrote Wells, the whole incident "was forgotten as one of the romances of the town."

Wells then fast-forwarded some twenty-five years to a time when he was in San Francisco on business. While there, he attended a benefit for "dependent girls" and found himself sitting across a table from a young couple, of which the female member was especially attractive and strangely familiar. He overheard them conversing about art and the philanthropic causes they believed in and concluded they were both educated and well-to-do. Wells avoided interrupting, but curiosity overtook him after he heard mention of Prescott. He began to informally interview the gentlewoman and learned that she'd indeed been born and raised in Prescott, Arizona, but landed in California after her father, Judge Charles Hall, sent her to Mills College in Oakland. Her name? C.C. Hall, short for Chance Cobweb Hall. How she received her unusual name, her father never told her: "I suppose that some kind of western romance was connected to it. Perhaps I will know sometime."[157]

With that, Wells ended his Chance Cobweb Hall chronicle.

THE TRUE STORY OF VIOLET "BABY BELL" HICKS

Rewinding to the night of Monday, January 17, 1898, the hot national topic was whether the United States should become militarily involved in the Cuban struggle for independence from Spanish rule. Bucky O'Neill was Prescott's mayor and just shy of seven months from striding fearlessly into immortality as a Rough Rider. Locally, people were still talking about the daring robbery that transpired at the Palace Saloon in the early morning of January 9. An eight month-old girl, however, was about to become "the sensation of the season."

As Wells asserted, it was an exceptionally cold, snowy night, and the saloons of Whiskey Row offered comfortable retreats. Cob Web Hall, which was indeed still extant, was probably as busy as any, but there wouldn't be a baby placed on its bar counter that night. That distinction would belong to the Cabinet Saloon. Although he had been proprietor of the Cob Web in the 1880s, Captain Fisher wasn't at the Cabinet or any other cantina that night. He'd died almost exactly nine years before. Colonel Bigelow was also a certain absentee, expiring in 1892. Theoretically, it's possible Robert Groom was present. Although he resided in Wickenburg during this time, he frequently visited Prescott while checking on nearby mines he owned. It's doubtful, however, that the seventy-three-year-old bachelor would've wanted to adopt and raise a baby.[158]

The Cabinet was now run by co-proprietors Ben Belcher and Barney Smith. Contrary to Wells's attestation, the night was not winding down. The clamor inherent to saloon life was at fever pitch. A high stakes faro game was still attracting the attention of many Cabinet patrons, and the soprano said to have retired for the night was still "hold[ing] sway on the stage at the rear of the saloon." In the midst of this civilized commotion, if anyone wanted to accomplish something surreptitious, now was the time.

There are no references to Belcher or Smith being present that night. It was their "genial mixologist" Frank Williams running the show—he plays counterpart to Captain Fisher of Wells's version. Naturally, he was keeping an eye on the Cabinet's bat-winged doors. His attention piqued when "a rather comely young woman" wearing a veil walked through them. But there was more; she was holding a swaddled baby. The mysterious lady promptly laid the bundle down, along with a note, on the bar counter and said something unintelligible to Williams. While making her getaway, the stunned bartender called out to her, "What does this all mean?" but she quickly disappeared into the darkness of Whiskey Row. A few nearby witnesses were moved when

Baby Bell was placed by "a rather comely young woman" on the end of this bar on January 17, 1898. *Sharlot Hall Museum.*

the child responded to his voice by extending a tiny hand and cooing as if to say, "Be my friend and shake." Fatherly instinct then seized Williams; he rushed out in search of nourishment for the cherub.

Meanwhile, all peripheral activities ceased as the precious waif magnetized everyone present. The baby's gender wasn't yet known, but the consensus was that it was a girl, and an exceptionally beautiful one. All were bewildered regarding its presence. Hence, another Cabinet employee stood above the crowd to clarify the situation by reading the note left behind, quoted here verbatim: "Mr. Saloon Keeper, Dear Sir—Here is a baby that belongs to William Bell, and he has left it on an invalid woman who has no one to do anything for her and is at this time sick in bed and his child is suffering for care and she has sent it down here to its father, hearing that he was there at your saloon of nights; and will you be so kind as to give the child in his hands or give it to the sheriff, for the woman is not able to keep the child nor cannot do it if he was paying her, but he does nothing for it."

As seen, Western saloon stories often result in drunken men pulling pistols and shooting at one another. This one is of a healthier variety. The *Courier* reported that "a surging mass of brawny men crowded up to get a sight of the little one." No less than forty were so taken with the infant— and undoubtedly inflicted with a benevolence supercharged by whiskey— that they volunteered to give it a home. A few married but childless men were even on the brink of fisticuffing for the tiny trophy. Things were getting out of control, so someone left to fetch Charles Hicks, probate judge of Yavapai County.

It's immediately clear that Hicks wasn't at the Cabinet when the baby was placed on the bar. One report conveyed that bartender Williams cared for the baby "until the arrival of Judge Hicks"; he wasn't already there waiting to gamble for possession of the child. The most trustworthy initial report tersely stated that at some point Hicks "finally captured the cherub and sent it home." Ten days later, the *Miner* iterated that the judge had indeed not only "been sent for" but, after appearing, "decided the question by announcing that he would take it himself." A refutation of Wells's assertion that the baby was an absolute stranger also appeared in the initial *Courier* report, citing that Hicks took it "home to its grandmother residing in West Prescott." The grandmother refused the child and provided some alibis for her daughter, and hence, the judge took the baby home to his wife, Allie.

What is known about the January 17 portion of this story ends there.[159]

Wells claimed the baby's biological parents were never known. Actually,

Charles Hicks was the probate judge of Yavapai County in 1898 and in charge of adoptions. *Sharlot Hall Museum.*

the father, William Bell, was identified immediately in the note left at the Cabinet. This made it easy to identify the mother, Mary Bell. Rumors swirled regarding her whereabouts. One was that she'd been sick in the county hospital but had returned to Jerome to work, leaving her baby with her mother, a Mrs. Harvey, in west Prescott. More likely, Mary and her daughter had been living with her mother all along but was now in hiding.

William Bell had indeed been seen frequenting the Cabinet "for some weeks" and had probably been there that day—he'd been seen in town. He may have even been at the Cabinet the very night his child was left on its bar counter. Regardless, somehow he learned of the incident and skipped town. A warrant for his arrest was immediately issued. The public learned on January 26 that "Wm. Bell, of Baby Bell fame, was brought in from Crowned King yesterday and lodged in jail."

Meanwhile, the Hickses were enjoying their new resident. According to the judge, "Baby Bell is one of the best babies in the country." He also divulged to the public the little one's gender for the first time: "She never cries at night and she is good all day long." The Hickses' bliss was interrupted when an unexpected visitor showed up at their door on January 26. It was Mary Bell, accompanied by her sister, claiming she'd come down from Jerome. She told the Hickses, probably after visiting William in jail, that neither she nor her husband desired to give up their daughter. As distressing as this must've been for the couple, they held their ground; they weren't willing to release the girl to either of her abandoners. The *Miner* was pleased to report, "Baby Bell will continue to remain an interesting occupant of the Hicks household for the present." Yet the child's future now seemed more in limbo than they'd hoped. To combat this, the judge shared a deleterious revelation about her mother: "She did not ask to see her progeny." On this day, surely after Mary Bell's visit, Allie Hicks petitioned for the adoption of Violet Bell.

On January 28, William and Mary Bell and Mrs. Harvey were standing before Justice Donald Campbell. It was Mr. Bell, however, on trial for failing to support his wife and daughter. Bell's defense was that he was jobless and having trouble finding work but while working he supported them. He then asserted that he cared for his daughter while also admitting he'd been away for months and contributed nothing toward her welfare. Bell's profession of parental love was discounted by an eyewitness to the trial: "His bearing was rather defiant, his tone and manner indicating that he felt like breaking out and had to struggle to control himself." This same onlooker questioned Bell's claim he couldn't find work, noting he was "a robust looking man of about 35 years of age." Campbell refused all excuses and gave Bell twenty-five days in jail.

Mary Bell—not appearing invalid as the note stated—was given every benefit of the doubt. No longer speaking on her estranged husband's behalf, she retracted, or at least clarified, half of what she told the Hickses and contradicted what was declared in the note left behind at the Cabinet. Mrs. Bell now testified that she expected financial support from Mr. Bell "*for the child only* [italics added]," and nothing more. This may have been enough to free her of abandonment charges but not with her expressed desire to reclaim custody of her baby girl.

On that same day, the Bells signed over their daughter to the Hickses. Violet Bell was now Violet Hicks. There can be little doubt that the adoption of Baby Bell was expedited because Charles Hicks was the probate judge of Yavapai County; probate judges handled all adoptions at this time in territorial history. Even more critical, both William and Mary Bell had abandoned their daughter, albeit in different ways. Mary Bell had dealt a hand against herself by allowing someone to deposit her baby on a saloon counter and leaving, or at least endorsing, a note relinquishing her role as mother. All in all, locals believed the adoption was for the best. The *Courier*— while also revealing the child's first name for the first time—stated it thus: "Thus has the little waif of the Cabinet saloon fallen into a home good enough for any child, one in which she will receive that care, training and education which any parents would be proud to have a child receive." The public drama of Violet "Baby Bell" Hicks ended there. Judge Wells's statement that it "was forgotten as one of the romances of the town" is true in the sense that it disappeared from the media.[160]

Of the many questions spawning from the night of January 17, 1898, two are most intriguing. First: Who was the mysterious lady who dropped Baby Bell off at the Cabinet Saloon? Only two suspects emerge: Mary Bell herself and her sister. The *Courier* referred to the person who deposited the baby on the saloon counter as a "rather comely young woman." Later, that same paper reported after the trial that Mrs. Bell was also not only "rather good looking" but also "appear[ed] to be about 20 years of age." It was clear what the *Courier* was inferring. Mary claimed she'd been sick when the baby was left on Whiskey Row, and afterward that she'd traveled to Jerome to work and then back to Prescott; these are not the actions of "an invalid woman." Given the tight chronology of events between January 17 and January 26—especially beginning with when Mary Bell visited the Hicks household—it appears likely these were simply alibis to avoid abandonment charges. Mary Bell surfaces as the most likely malefactor. Second: Were men gambling for the right to adopt Baby Bell when Judge Hicks arrived? Evidence suggests that although they might not have been gambling to adopt Violet, they were indeed gambling and anteing money "for the child's benefit." Two outside reports indicate that Hicks took not only the baby with him but also $300. Charity on Whiskey Row was not unheard of.[161]

Very little is known about Violet Hicks's childhood. She revealed a bare minimum to her children about her past. Her son, Chester Binner—the youngest of her four children—remembered his mother sharing that she had learned to ride a horse before she could walk. She'd also been fond

Tragically, Baby Bell's adopted mother, Allie Hicks, died two years after Arizona's most famous saloon incident transpired. *Bradley G. Courtney.*

of a Chinese cook who resided in the Hicks household. That was about it. Chester, although he knew his mother was adopted, didn't learn about the Cabinet Saloon incident of January 17, 1898, until 1999. Sadly, Violet never knew her adopted mother. Allie Hicks died on February 7, 1900.

In 1972, a pulp Western history magazine called *Frontier Times* spoke of rumors that C.C. Hall, under an assumed name, was living anonymously in the shadows of Whiskey Row. This was never true. Her adult life was far less magic than tragic. At some point, Violet moved to California, just as Wells said. There's no record that she ever attended Mills College, an all-girls school, as Wells claimed, but she did attend an art school in San Francisco. There she met her future husband, Arthur Binner Jr., who would become a successful architectural sculptor. Early in their marriage, they lived in Oakland. For a while, they were happy together and with their four children; her son even remarked that Violet was "a great mother in my early life."

Things began to unravel when Arthur started drinking. By the time Chester turned four years old, Arthur started beating Violet and became abusive even to the extent of expressing murderous intentions toward his children. At some point in 1929, Violet obtained a restraining order. Arthur then cut off financial support. Her adopted father visited her about this time and stayed for several weeks, surely to try to improve his beloved daughter's situation, as he'd always done. It was the last time they'd be together. Charles Hicks died in Prescott on Christmas Eve 1929, shortly after his visit with Violet. His adopted daughter attended his funeral. Violet's son recalled that his mother believed her worries were over after learning the former judge had owned some gold mines. She thought she would receive a sizable inheritance. Chester explained, however, that Hicks hadn't "[kept] up the assay payments, or something, and [Violet] didn't get any inheritance at all. She came back home disgusted."

After her husband left and Charles Hicks passed, Violet became not only sad and bitter but also a gambling addict. Chester professed that his mother spent a lot of time at the racetrack: "When she won she took us to the circus, and when she lost the landlord was pounding on the door." There were times, he recalled, when there was nothing more to eat than a single onion.

Violet was able to reconnect with her mother, Mary Bell, and establish a good relationship. Sadly, after trekking all the way to Alaska to find her father, William Bell, she was informed he wanted nothing to do with her. His abandonment was total. Although to a lesser degree, Violet became a deserter of progeny as well, kicking Chester out of the house when he was seventeen because she could no longer feed him. She died in 1970 at the age of seventy-two. Chester didn't learn of it until months later.[162]

Why are there so many discrepancies between Edmund Wells's Chance Cobweb Hall saga and the true story of Violet Hicks? Was it simply a case of a senile eighty-something-year-old man confusing and/or forgetting the facts? The answer is: most certainly not. *Argonaut Tales* is too well written, lucid, creative and, at times, philosophical. The mind that penned it was clearly operating at a high level. Evidence allows for an inference that Wells knew the true story of Violet Hicks and purposely altered it; it served as the framework for a sensational western frontier story. Wells and Charles Hicks were well acquainted and may have even been close personal friends. Both were judges, but even more revealing, when a young Charles Hicks first arrived in the Prescott area in 1880, his first employer was none other than Edmund Wells.

It's not difficult to deduce that Wells, in the interest of protecting Hicks and his adopted daughter, camouflaged the true story. Indeed, being abandoned by both biological parents could have an adverse psychological effect on an individual, not to mention knowing it included being coldly deposited on a frontier town saloon counter. It's possible she never knew how she'd come to be adopted. Except for Chester when he was an older man, her children never knew their mother was Whiskey Row's famous "baby on the bar." As seen, Wells's "C.C. Hall" character never knew the origin of her name. Interestingly, there was a well-known traveling businessman from Albuquerque who visited Prescott often. His name was C.C. Hall. Was Wells communicating an inside joke with Prescottonians by using that name in *Argonaut Tales*?[163]

For serious historians or those who simply love history, it's important to acknowledge there is a place for legend and folklore, popular history and anti-footnoters and even historical fiction. They make the truly curious seek true, scholarship-oriented history. Yet, it is human nature to try to make something beautiful out of something not so beautiful. Addressing this matter, an overall warning regarding *Argonaut Tales* was issued by none other than Arizona's most celebrated poetess and lady historian, Sharlot Hall. In a review of Wells's book before it was available to the general public, she cautioned future readers: "It is not all history, not meant to be all history." Then to substantiate the value of literature akin to *Argonaut Tales*, she added, "The pages that are pure romance are perhaps more true and valuable than the ones that are history verified—just as a man's dreams are more true and permanently valuable than his every-day life."[164]

It's equally human to dig deep for historical truth, knowing that, while it might not be what was hoped for, it's still a treasure chest from which to learn. The most obvious lesson extracted from the Violet "Baby Bell" Hicks story is that abandonment by one's biological parents is a formidable psychological hurdle to overcome, even after experiencing a special love from surrogate parents. The true history of Violet Bell, aka Violet Hicks and Violet Binner, is one that began with a turmoil she was too young to remember yet led to a childhood whereby she experienced advantages many children of her time would not. As an adult, she reverted to domestic chaos and a personal life marked by sadness and bitterness. The legend of Chance Cobweb Hall would prove the better choice for a movie version of this story.

Chapter 11

Buckey O'Neill, the Rough Riders and Whiskey Row

William "Buckey" O'Neill is perhaps historic Prescott's most famous and revered citizen. He was also one of Whiskey Row's most devoted customers. Buckey seemed to lead a charmed life and had a knack for stepping into the middle of historic events. Starting in 1882, after departing Tombstone, where he worked for the *Tombstone Epitaph* during the days of Wyatt Earp and Doc Holliday, the well-educated, charismatic O'Neill became one of the row's biggest stars until leaving it in 1898 to fight in the Spanish-American War as a member of the legendary Rough Riders. Today, a statue representing him riding a rearing stallion stands majestically like a sentinel in the Courthouse Plaza. O'Neill was a natural leader and nervously energetic go-getter with an ambition that went beyond a quest for success. Buckey yearned for glory. When he discovered the Whiskey Row way of life, the risk-taker surfaced time and time again, so much so that detractors saw his gambling as an addiction. He'd earned the nickname "Buckey" before he hit twenty years of age in the gambling halls of Phoenix, where he became a gambling hall legend playing his favorite game, faro. Faro was wildly popular in the 1800s because a player's odds for winning were higher than in other card games. On the back of some faro cards was an illustration of a tiger, and sometimes just the act of playing a faro game was called "bucking the tiger." Sometimes it meant a player going for broke and betting it all. The latter meaning applied to the gutsy William O'Neill, who became "Buckey" because of it.

Buckey came to Prescott in 1882. For sixteen years, he continued to buck the tiger on Whiskey Row and always with a cigarette dangling from his mouth. At first, it was usually in the Cabinet, Diana or Sazerac saloons and then later in the Palace after it became more prominent. The chain-smoking O'Neill at first worked as a court reporter for the *Miner* before starting his own newspaper, *Hoof and Horn*, which ran for four years. In 1886, he was made captain of the local militia, the Prescott Grays. That same year, he ran for political office for the first time, that of probate judge and superintendent of schools. Being a well-known Whiskey Row habitué led some adversaries to run a smear campaign against him. Buckey was portrayed as a reckless gambler and drunkard: "Though young in years, his bleared eye and flushed face give evidence that the nights of dissipation—the days of continuous drunks—are slowly but surely undermining a naturally strong and vigorous constitution." These attacks backfired and instead made him more appealing to the common man. Buckey won the election. Next came a two-year stint as Yavapai County sheriff. Before he rode into immortality as a Rough Rider, O'Neill was elected mayor of Prescott in 1897.

In the spring of 1889, four cowhands from the famous Hashknife outfit near the Little Colorado River in northern Arizona robbed a train near Diablo Canyon. Buckey, as sheriff, led a three-man posse that chased the outlaws relentlessly through rugged areas on the Navajo Indian Reservation and as far up as Lee's Ferry on the Colorado River and through parts of Glen Canyon. The chase was almost three weeks long but ended with a successful capture, which guaranteed Buckey a place in Arizona history.

The captured men were taken to Salt Lake City and deposited on a train to Prescott. Along the way, one prisoner, J.J. Smith, escaped. Buckey went

Buckey O'Neill enjoyed gambling and drinking in the Cabinet and Palace saloons, seen here from Cortez Street in the 1890s. *Sharlot Hall Museum.*

after him, solo, but after six hours gave up and returned to the train. The remaining three prisoners were tried in Prescott, convicted and sentenced to twenty-five years in the Yuma Territorial Prison. At some point, Smith was recaptured in Texas near the Oklahoma border and hauled to Prescott. Buckey had to collect Smith's partners in Yuma for his trial, which he did by train. When they arrived in Prescott, the famous Canyon Diablo train robbery soon became a Whiskey Row story.

Bill Crocker was a boy when the convicts arrived in Prescott. A large crowd had gathered at the depot to get another glimpse of the infamous trio. When it came time to take the prisoners to the county courthouse jail, they were posited into an open carriage. The feisty Crocker jumped on the back and rode right up to the courthouse steps, which earned him a front-row view of the bad men. Crocker, during an interview years later at St. Michael's Hotel, related, "One of the robbers, irritated by all the attention they were receiving, lashed out with his foot and gave me a kick in the pants and swearing at me to, 'Get the hell out of here.'"

Buckey had heard rumors that the robbers' friends were going to attempt to liberate them. During the evening of November 19, 1898, he placed extra guards around the jail and sent extra watchmen to patrol Whiskey Row. The manner in which this jailbreak was attempted came as a surprise and hence wasn't associated with it immediately. Some saw it as a freak occurrence that established a record for Prescott: three fires in four hours. Around six o'clock, the first alarm sounded. A fire had been spotted behind the Palace Saloon, then being run by D.C. Thorne. After the incipient flames were suffocated, the first red flag was discovered. Beneath floor level were areas saturated with coal oil, which some surmised as having come from an exploded lamp. Not police chief James Dodson, however, whose suspicion was aroused immediately. Within forty-five minutes of the first fire and less than one hundred feet away, a second fire was spotted in Whiskey Row Alley behind D. Levy's store. It, too, was quickly subdued. Three hours later, around 10:15 p.m., another alarm. Sloan's Plaza Stable on Goodwin Street was ablaze. The flames were already shooting through the stable's roof. The opera house adjoined to it also caught fire and couldn't be saved, but the fire stopped there. One report claimed that eighteen horses perished. It quickly became a theory that the fires were set hoping to draw Buckey and his guards away from the jail. O'Neill didn't bite, and no escapes were made. Bill Crocker later stated, "They placed oil soaked rags under many of the business houses ON Whiskey Row. If Smith's friends had succeeded in setting all the fires [they had planned to set], Prescott would have had its big fire ten years sooner."

Theodore Roosevelt spawned the idea of raising "a regiment of cowboys and mounted riflemen," which became famous as the Rough Riders. *Wikimedia Commons.*

Smith was sentenced to thirty years in prison, but the incendiaries were never caught. Locals were especially angry because horses had died in such a horrible way. O'Neill was charged with bringing the four prisoners to Yuma. He enlisted James Dodson to help him with the escort. Crocker noted, "Realizing the type of men with whom they had to travel, the train robbers created no disturbance and were delivered without disturbance."[165]

After his two-year term as sheriff, Buckey endeavored in several fields, including white onyx mining (which made him wealthy) and the hotel business (he and wife, Pauline, bought a two-thirds interest in the Burke Hotel). In 1898, he was elected mayor of Prescott. Within months, President William McKinley decided that America should intervene in Cuba's struggle for independence from Spain. Buckey wasn't willing to allow a chance to fight in such a righteous war to slip by. Under Secretary of the Navy Theodore Roosevelt felt the same way. Roosevelt's idea was to enlist frontier-hardened men from the Indian Territory: Arizona, New Mexico, Texas and Oklahoma. Presidential authorization was eventually given "to raise a regiment of cowboys and mounted riflemen." Buckey was the first to volunteer. Governor Myron McCord appointed Buckey captain of one troop. Soon he was recruiting men between eighteen and forty-five years old, all experienced horsemen and marksmen.

Potential recruits came to Prescott from all over Yavapai County and Arizona. Whiskey Row suddenly became the most popular locale in the Southwest. It's been rumored that some recruits visited every saloon in one day before heading off to Texas for boot camp. The Palace, however, was a particular favorite. Bob Brow demonstrated especially strong support for the volunteers and their cause by providing them a troop mascot, a mountain lion named Florence. It wasn't the first time Brow had a wildcat in the Palace. In 1894, he had one that escaped to be with his "brethren" on the outside but returned to its cage asking to be fed when things didn't go well out in the wild. During the war, Brow kept Palace patrons informed regarding how "Teddy's Terrors" were faring by illustrating "so strikingly real and artistically" each important event on a blackboard. This drew a continually large crowd.

The send-off given to the boys was Prescott's biggest event to date. The troopers, to the sight of waving handkerchiefs and flags and the sound of boisterous cheers, marched up Montezuma Street to the train depot, where they loaded up on four Santa Fe, Prescott and Phoenix Railroad cars. As they pulled away, Prescottonians serenaded them with all of their hearts, "God Be With You Till We Meet Again." It would be the last time Buckey would see

On July 3, 1907, a huge crowd gathered to witness the unveiling of the Rough Rider Monument, also known as the Buckey O'Neill Monument. *Nancy Burgess.*

Cheers erupted when Buckey's stepson, Maurice, yanked the ropes, releasing the shroud that unveiled one of Solon Borglum's finest works. *Nancy Burgess.*

Prescott and Whiskey Row. Leading his men just before the Rough Riders made their famous charges up Kettle and San Juan Hills, a Spanish bullet he'd said he was immune to struck him down. Colonel Roosevelt wrote, "As he turned on his heel a bullet struck him in the mouth and came out at the back of his head, so that even before he fell his wild and gallant soul had gone out into the darkness."[166]

In the spring of 1899, Buckey O'Neill's body was recovered and sailed back to the United States. On May 1, he was buried with honors in the Arlington National Cemetery. To Prescottonians, however, Buckey remained one of theirs. In 1905, Solon Borglum, brother of the Mount Rushmore National Memorial sculptor, was commissioned to create a bronze statue that would commemorate Captain O'Neill and the Rough Riders who fought with him. On July 3, 1907, seven thousand people gathered around the cloaked monument after a mile-long parade that included some Rough Riders. Cheers erupted when Buckey's stepson, Maurice, yanked the ropes, releasing the shroud that unveiled one of Borglum's finest works: a straining stallion being reined by a cowboy-looking soldier. Today, when visitors ask who that man is, there is usually a Prescottonian nearby who will explain, "That's Bucky O'Neill, a Rough Rider who rode with Theodore Roosevelt and one of the greatest heroes of our town."[167]

Chapter 12

Prelude to the Death of Whiskey Row

Whiskey Row was relatively peaceful in 1899, and Prescott was in the midst of a fluid conversion phase from town to city. The year 1900 in America found William McKinley serving as America's president and campaigning for reelection. Less than two years before, Colonel Theodore Roosevelt, against seemingly impossible odds, had led the Rough Riders up the Cuban hills of Kettle and San Juan during the Spanish-American War. His political career rocketed after these heroics. Now the governor of New York and beloved in Prescott, Roosevelt was expected to become McKinley's running mate. This didn't stop the Democrat's presidential nominee, William Jennings Bryan, from making a campaign stop in Prescott in 1900. The renowned orator, who had stumped in Prescott for the same reason four years earlier, visited again in mid-April during a train tour. Prescottonians called the event "Bryan Day." Bryan gave his speech in front of the courthouse, near where the Buckey O'Neill statue stands today. In March, long-distance telephoning had been established between Prescott and Phoenix. One witness was astonished, as anyone with proper sensibilities would've been, that "their voices were easily recognizable and their articulation could be heard as distinctly as though they were standing only a few feet [from] the person addressing them instead of being over 100 miles away."[168]

Unlike most American climatic milieus whereby "April showers bring May flowers," April and May in the Central Arizona Highlands are the third and second sparsest months respectively regarding rainfall. The lowest? June. The spring and early summer of 1900 had been drier than usual.

Democratic presidential candidate William Jennings Bryan stumped in Prescott in 1900 during a train tour. *Library of Congress.*

Concern regarding the Prescott drought became so great that on May 21, mayor pro tem Fred Brecht issued an emergency edict that continued to be published right up until July 14. Water was obviously needed for drinking, plumbing and irrigation. It was also needed, God forbid, to extinguish fires. A ban was enacted regarding the use of water for the watering of lawns and gardens, the exception being in the evening hours between seven and eight o'clock.[169]

Time marched on. Spring fluxed into summer. Still no rain. The middle of June found Mayor John Dougherty back in town. Early on he visited his brother, Joe, who owned a grocery store located on one of the corners of Gurley and Granite Streets. An argument between the brothers was overheard by an employee, Bert Lee. Joe was not pleased that his mayor/ brother and the Prescott City Council seemed more concerned about the town's physical appearance than its physical safety. Ironically, an unusually wet winter had left the streets of Prescott in a state that was "by no means in a very presentable condition." A decision had been made by the local government to spend available funds to grade the streets rather than find a way to increase Prescott's water supply. Joe argued, "Why the hell do you have to grade the streets right now? If you're short of money, what you got ought to do is deepen those wells or dig new ones. What if we have a fire—how'd you stop it?" The mayor fired back that there was sufficient water to handle whatever problems may arise. The incredulous grocer retorted that "there wasn't enough water to put out a chicken coop if it was on fire." On July 3, John Dougherty's decision to pave the streets provided the locals a false dash of hope: "There was a slight sprinkle that occurred up and down Montezuma street yesterday afternoon, but it came from Arizona Paving Co.'s water cart."[170]

When the Saturday evening of July 14 rolled around, the people of Prescott were in an especially festive mood. The Courthouse Plaza teemed

This rare image shows what Whiskey Row looked like circa 1900. *Nancy Burgess.*

A miner's candleholder, like the one pictured here, is said to be behind Whiskey Row's Great Fire of 1900. (Miner's candleholder courtesy of John McKinney). *Norman Fisk.*

with people hoping the summer night would cool. The saloons were packed. Sheriff George Ruffner patrolled the scene and said to "jail all the drunks in Prescott tonight you'd have to put a roof over the whole town." That day, four miners, said to be Italian, had rented a room at the OK Lodging House for one dollar. They'd been drinking in the recently reopened bar located on the first floor of the Scopel Hotel on the corner of Goodwin and Montezuma Streets. Jake Weber was the saloon manager. That night, people in Weber's bar were drinking more than usual, so much so that he had to rush over to Jake Marks's liquor store on Gurley Street to buy more booze. At some point before ten o'clock, the miners decided to retire. Upon returning to their room, however, they decided the night was still young and that they needed to drink more. They would need light when they came back, so one of the miners lit a candle, placed it on a miner's candleholder and jabbed it into the wall. As the boys drank in Weber's saloon, the candle burned until it eventually became unclamped and fell on a nearby bed.[171]

Like the modern-day "Big One," when the San Andreas Fault finally makes that promised big slip and imposes its long-predicted destruction, a big fire in Prescott was not a question of "If?" but "When?" And so it was on July 14, 1900. Whiskey Row would be wiped out in a matter of hours. The Great Fire of 1900 would prove the pivotal event in Prescott and its famous row's history. That's a story worthy of a fuller telling.

Notes

Chapter 1

1. *The Arizona Miner* (hereafter cited as *Miner*), March 9 and July 20, 1864; Al Bates, *Territorial Times* 7, no. 2 (Prescott Corral of the Westerners): 4–7, 22–28.
2. Jan MacKell Collins, *Wild Women of Prescott, Arizona* (Charleston: The History Press, 2015): 13, 17–18.
3. Isaac Goldberg, "Reminiscences of a Pioneer," *Arizona Historical Review* 2, no. 3 (October 1929): 91–92.
4. *Miner*, September 21, 1864.
5. "Barnard, George W.," vertical/surname file, Sharlot Hall Museum Library and Archives, Prescott (hereafter cited as SHML&A).
6. Alfred Banta, undated editorial, *St. Johns (AZ) Observer*; *Miner*, July 6 and August 24, 1864.
7. *Prescott Courier* (hereafter cited as *Courier*), August 19, 1911.
8. Banta from undated *Observer*.
9. *Miner*, July 6, 1864.
10. "Genung, Charles B.," 2, Sharlot Hall Collection, series 3-1, Local History Notes, box 10.3, SHML&A.
11. *Miner*, October 26, 1864, and March 9, 1877.
12. Ibid., September 1, 1876.

Chapter 2

13. Ibid., September 20, 1868, and March 9, 1877.
14. Ibid., September 21, 1864.
15. Ibid., October 5, 1864.

16. Philip D. Yeder, "The History of Fort Whipple," unpublished thesis, SHML&A, 28; *Miner*, November 23, 1864.

17. *Miner*, November 23, 1864; William Boyd Finch, "William Claude Jones: The Charming Rogue Who Named Arizona," *Journal of Arizona History* 31, no. 4: 415.

18. "Bourke, John P.," vertical/surname file, SHML&A.

19. *Miner*, December 14, 1864.

20. Charles C. Niehuis, "Whiskey Row: Portrait of a Street," *Arizona Highways*, October 1938.

21. *Miner*, October 4, 1865.

22. Yeder, *History of Fort Whipple*, 26–27.

23. *Miner*, June 15, 1867.

24. Ibid., April 1, 1871.

25. "Noyes, Albert Osgood," vertical/surname file, 1, and letter from Noyes to Olivia, July 2, 1868, SHML&A.

26. *Courier*, July 8, 1898.

27. *Miner*, July 30, 1870.

28. Ibid., July 4 and August 22, 1868.

29. Ibid., August 15, 1868.

30. Ibid., September 5, 1868.

31. Ibid., October 3, and November 7, 1868.

32. "Moeller, Andrew," vertical/surname file, SHML&A; Tom Collins, "Andrew L. Moeller: Pioneer, Entrepreneur, Philanthropist," Days Past Archives, March 27, 2010, SHML&A; *Miner*, August 3, 1877; *Clifton Clarion*, February 4, 1885.

33. *Miner*, November 21, 1868.

34. Ibid., November 28, 1868.

35. Ibid., December 12, 1868.

36. Ibid., September 25, 1869.

37. Ibid., October 16 and 23, 1869.

38. Ibid., March 11, 1871.

CHAPTER 3

39. Ibid., January 28, 1871.

40. Ibid., March 13 and December 11, 1869.

41. Ibid., July 2 and 9, 1870.

42. Ibid., October 8 and November 12, 1870.

43. Ibid., August 6, 1870, and April 4. 1871.

44. Ibid., March 25, April 12, June 10, October 22, November 12 and December 3, 1870.

45. Ibid., December 11, 1869.

46. Ibid., March 8, 1873.

47. Ibid., July 13, 1872.

48. Ibid., January 28, 1871.

49. Ibid., November 9, 1877.

50. Ibid., April 14 and July 1, 1879.

51. Ibid., November 25, 1881.
52. *Courier*, September 23 and 30, 1882.
53. Ibid., October 2, 1892; *Miner*, October 3, 1892.

CHAPTER 4

54. "Thorne, D. C.," vertical/surname file, SHML&A.
55. Map 18, SHML&A.
56. "Thorne," SHML&A.
57. *Miner*, January 1, April 2 and June 18, 1870.
58. Ibid., December 30 and March 28, 1913.
59. "Thorne," SHML&A; R. Michael Wilson, *Encyclopedia of Stage Coach Robberies in Arizona* (Las Vegas: RaMa Press, 2003): 172–73.
60. *Miner*, August 24, 1877.
61. Ibid., August 17, 1877.
62. Ibid., June 29, 1877.
63. Ibid., September 28, 1877.
64. Ibid., December 29, 1876.

CHAPTER 5

65. Ibid., January 24, February 14 and August 22, 1866; and May 4, 1867.
66. Ibid., February 28, May 9 and October 27, 1866; March 31, 1868; February 5, 1870; and March 10, 1876.
67. Ibid., December 31, 1875.
68. Ibid., April 21, 1876.
69. *Courier*, July 21, 1883; February 23 and July 4, 1884.
70. Ibid., October 13, 1883.
71. Ibid., November 10, 1883.
72. *Miner*, November 9, 1883.
73. Ibid., November 9, 1883; *Courier*, November 10, 17 and 24, 1883; January 12 and 26, 1884.
74. *Miner*, February 1, 1888; *Courier*, November 7, 1890, and February 16, 1891.
75. *Miner*, October 24, 1868.
76. Ibid., February 6, 1869.
77. Ibid., August 30, 1873.
78. Ibid., October 19, 1877.
79. Ibid., October 19 and 26, 1877.
80. Ibid., November 19, 1880.
81. Ibid., November 30, 1877; *Courier*, September 9, 1882.
82. *Courier*, December 18, 1885; Obit Book, 460, SHML&A.
83. *Miner*, November 17, 1886, and July 13, 1887.
84. Ibid., October 30, November 20 and 27, 1895.
85. "Fires," vertical file, 20, SHML&A.

CHAPTER 6

86. *Miner*, May 15 and August 21, 1869.

87. Ibid., May 14, 1870.

88. Ibid., June 24, 1881; *Courier*, November 18, 1882; Ed Sipos, *Brewing Arizona* (Tucson: University of Arizona Press, 2013): 52.

89. *Courier*, September 9, 1882.

90. *Miner*, May 10, 1878, and May 23, 1879.

91. Ibid., October 25, 1878.

92. Ibid., November 17, 1867.

93. Ibid., July 2 and November 26, 1880; April 22, 1881.

94. Ibid., November 26, 1880; March 25, April 22 and July 22, 1881.

95. Ibid., March 25, 1881.

96. *Courier*, August 19 and 22, 1882; May 22, 1888; *Miner*, December 21, 1887.

97. *Courier*, September 8, 1883.

98. Ibid., March 15 and June 20, 1884; *Miner*, July 25, 1884.

99. *Miner*, December 17, 1875.

100. Ibid., September 1, 1876.

101. Ibid., December 1, 1876.

102. *Courier*, October 27, 1883.

103. *Miner*, weekly advertisements in 1875.

104. *Miner*, February 6, 1880; February 24 and March 3, 1882; *Courier*, March 4, 1882.

105. *Miner*, March 3, April 21 and June 30, 1882; Obit Book, 16, SHML&A.

106. *Miner*, June 10, 1891; "Places and Things: Robberies," vertical file, SHML&A.

107. *Miner*, July 25, 1884; Edmund Wells, *Argonaut Tales: Stories of the Gold Seekers and the Indian Scouts of Early Arizona* (New York: Frederick H. Hitchcock/The Grafton Press, 1927): 215.

108. *Miner*, December 13, 1878, and September 12, 1879.

109. Ibid., July 4, 1879; *Courier*, October 27 and December 8, 1883; January 14, 1887.

CHAPTER 7

110. *Miner*, March 15 and April 5, 1878; April 4 and October 17, 1879.

111. Ibid., March 10, 1876; October 1, 1880; March 3, May 20 and December 30, 1882.

112. Ibid., March 26, 1880; March 25 and August 19, 1881; May 20, 1882.

113. Ibid., May 26 and December 24, 1880.

114. Ibid., January 21, 1881.

115. Ibid., December 23 and 30, 1881.

116. Ibid., June 7 and 21, April 25, 1879.

117. Ibid., June 21 and August 23, 1878; August 19, 1881; March 3. 1882.

118. Ibid., April 30, 1880.

119. *Courier*, December 19, 1891.

120. Ibid., September 9, 1882; January 5, 1882; September 13 and October 17, 1887; *Miner*, July 23, 1880; and October 1, 1881.

121. Letter to A.L. Dodson from Homer Wood, December 13, 1947, SHML&A; *Miner*, May 13, 1881; February 10 and 17, 1882.

122. *Miner*, August 4, 1879.

123. Ibid., March 5, 1880, and March 3, 1883.

124. Ibid., December 2, 1881.

125. Ibid., May 13, 1881.

126. Ibid., July 15, 1881.

127. Ibid., February 10 and 17, 1882.

128. *Courier*, April 1, 1881; *Miner*, April 17, 1881.

129. *Courier*, April 17, 1885, July 31, 1885, and October 12, 1887.

130. *Miner*, May 16 and July 1, 1881; June 16, 1883; and June 8, 1886.

131. Ibid., February 9, 1898; *Courier*, January 7, 1891, and April 12, 1895.

Chapter 8

132. *Miner*, June 22, 1877, December 9, 1881.

133. John C. Hazeltine to Madison Loring, April 15, 1955, in "Hazeltine Family," vertical/surname file, SHML&A; Paul Hughes, *Bank Notes* (Phoenix: Phoenician Books, 1971): 29.

134. *Miner*, December 30, 1881; December 31, 1882; April 14 and May 26, 1883; *Courier*, March 4, 1882.

135. *Courier*, June 6, 1883.

136. Ibid., June 30 and August 18, 1883.

137. *Miner*, September 21, 1877; January 20 and April 5, 1882; *Courier*, March 11, 1882.

138. *Courier*, July 7, 1883; *Miner*, November 26, 1870, and January 28, 1871.

Chapter 9

139. *Courier*, March 20, 1885; *Miner*, October 17, November 9, 1883, and October 3, 1884.

140. *Miner*, February 15, 1884; *Courier*, February 23, 1884.

141. *Courier*, February 24, March 22 and 29, 1884.

142. *Miner*, July 4 and 11, 1884.

143. Ken Edwards, "'Murder' in the Palace Saloon," unpublished manuscript, 1–2; *Courier*, September 5, 1884; "MURDERS #1," vertical file, uncited newspaper clipping, SHML&A.

144. Edwards, "Murder," 4, 6–8; *Courier*, January 15, 1891; *Miner*, January 21, 1891.

145. *Miner*, November 30, 1883; *Courier*, March 27, July 10, July 31, September 18, October 9, January 9 and November 20, 1885.

146. *Courier*, October 1 and October 15, 1886.

147. *Miner*, April 4 and May 2, 1888; Fred Veil, "The Legend of Kissing Jenny," Days Past Archives, March 30, 2013, SHML&A; Barry Goldwater to Tom Sullivan, August 10, 1977, SHML&A.

148. *Miner*, January 30, 1889.

149. *Courier*, August 25, 1888, and June 3, 1892; *Miner*, September 30, 1892, and June 22, 1896.

150. *Miner*, November 15, 22 and 29, December 13, 1893; January 3, February 21 and 28, 1894; Melissa Ruffner, *Prescott: A Pictorial History* (Prescott: Primrose Press, 1981): 74.

151. *Miner*, November 10 and 17, 1897.

152. Ibid., December 29, 1897.

153. Ibid., July 1, 1896; *Courier*, July 3, 1896.

154. *Miner*, July 22, 1896.

155. Ibid., January 12, 1898; *Courier*, January 14, 1898.

CHAPTER 10

156. Paul G. Rosenblatt, "Edmund W. Wells: Arizona Argonaut and Much More," *Territorial Times* 5, no. 2 (May 2012): 9–14; "Wells, Edmund W." vertical/surname file, SHML&A.

157. Wells, *Argonaut Tales*, 214–51.

158. *Miner*, January 9, 1889; December 21, 1892; and December 8, 1897.

159. "Hall, Chance Cobweb," vertical/surname file, SHML&A; *Miner*, January 19 and 26, 1898; *Courier*, January 21, 1898.

160. *Miner*, January 26 and February 2, 1898; *Courier*, January 28 and February 1, 1898.

161. *Courier*, January 21 and February 21, 1898; *Irrigation Age* 12, no. 5 (Chicago: February 1898): 140; Uncited newspaper clipping dated January 16, 1898, "Arizona Pioneers Remembrance Book," 47.

162. Roland Schmidt, "Booze, Bets and Babes: Gay and Gory Episodes on Whiskey Row," *Frontier Times*, February–March 1972: 13, 69; Chester Binner, interviewed by Leo Banks, August 16 and September 14, 1999, "Hall, Chance Cobweb," 1–3; *Miner*, February 14, 1900; *Courier*, December 24, 1929.

163. *Courier*, September 21, 1894.

164. Sharlot Hall, "'Argonaut Tales' Written by Judge Wells Wins High Praise from Sharlot Hall," *Arizona Republican*, April 22, 1928.

CHAPTER 11

165. *Courier*, November 19, 1898; William Crocker to Mrs. Metzger, April 15, 1957, Data Box 17, Folder 1, SHML&A.

166. Dale L. Walker, *Rough Rider: Buckey O'Neill of Arizona* (Lincoln: University of Nebraska Press, 1997): 124–32, 171–75; Charles H. Herner, "Arizona's Cowboys Cavalry," *Arizoniana* 5, no. 4 (Winter 1964): 19; *Miner*, August 29, 1894; *Miner*, April 25, 1898.

167. Walker, *Rough Rider*, 179–80, 185–86.

CHAPTER 12

168. *Miner*, March 7 and April 17, 1900.

169. *Courier*, June 2, 1900.

170. Pat Savage, *One Last Frontier: A Story of Indians, Early Settlers, and Old Ranches of Northern Arizona* (New York: Exposition Press, 1964): 217; *Miner*, January 17, 1900.

171. Toni and Robert McInnes, "George C. Ruffner: Frontier Sheriff, Yavapai County," *Sheriff Magazine*, August 1950.

About the Author

Bradley G. Courtney is an independent historian who lived and taught in Phoenix, Arizona, for nineteen years, and on the Navajo Indian Reservation in northern Arizona for twelve years. For six of those years, he was also a riverboat pilot and guide who gave tours down the incomparable canyons of the Colorado River. Brad has also recorded three albums of original music and has appeared on CNN, the Travel Channel and numerous other television stations across the country. He holds a master's degree in history from California State University. Brad served as sheriff of the award-winning Prescott Corral of Westerners International in 2015. He and his wife, Holly, now live near Prescott, Arizona, in the beautiful Prescott National Forest.